A Mother's Advice

KING LEMUEL AND HIS MOTHER:

The Exegesis of a Text: The Proverbial Woman Proverbs 31

CARLOTTA MARIA SHINN-RUSSELL

SHINN
RUSSELL
BOOKS & PUBLICATIONS

A Mother's Advice

KING LEMUEL AND HIS MOTHER:

The Exegesis of a Text:
The Proverbial Woman: Proverbs 31

CARLOTTA MARIA SHINN-RUSSELL

TABLE OF CONTENTS

PART I:
JUDGING RIGHTEOUSLY
PROVERBS 31:1-9

PART II:
THE PRICE OF A VIRTUOUS WOMAN:
PROVERBS 31:10-14

PART III:
A WOMAN CARES FOR HER FAMILY
PROVERBS 31:15-19

PART IV:
THE VIRTUOUS WOMAN HELPS THE NEEDY
PROVERBS 31:20-25

PART V:
THE VIRTUOUS WOMAN SPEAKS WISDOM
PROVERBS 31:26-31

WISDOM

"*Let not mercy and truth forsake thee: bind them about thy neck; write them upon the table of thine heart: So shalt thou find favour and good understanding in the sight of God and man. Trust in the Lord with all thine heart; and lean not unto thine own understanding. In all thy ways acknowledge him, and he shall direct thy paths. Be not wise in thine own eyes: fear the Lord and depart from evil. It shall be health to thy navel, and marrow to thy bones. Honour the Lord with thy substance, and with the first fruits of all thine increase: So, shall thy barns be filled with plenty, and thy presses shall burst out with new wine,*" [Proverbs 3:3–10].

"*Happy is the man that findeth wisdom, and the man that getteth understanding. For the merchandise of it is better than the merchandise of silver, and the gain thereof than fine gold. She is more precious than rubies: and all the things thou canst desire are not to be compared unto her. Length of days is in her right hand, and in her left-hand riches and honour. Her ways are ways of pleasantness, and all her paths are peace. She is a tree of life to them that lay hold upon her: and happy is everyone that retaineth her,*" [Proverbs 3:13–18].

"*Thus, saith the Lord, let not the wise man glory in his wisdom, neither let the mighty man glory in his might, let not the rich man glory in his riches: but let him that glorieth glory in this, that he understandeth and knoweth Me, that I am the Lord which exercise lovingkindness, judgment, and righteousness, in the earth: for in these things I delight, saith the Lord,*" [Jeremiah 9:23–24].

Christ offers Zion, why stay in Babylon? – The Church opposed to the World.

There is joy in walking in Christ while here on Earth.

Unbelief and disobedience have dreadful consequences: it is out of our own zeal that we reject Christ.

"*Who can find a virtuous woman? for her price is far above rubies. The heart of her husband doth safely trust in her, so that he shall have no need of spoil; she will do him good and not evil all the days of her life,*" [Proverbs 31:10-12].

"*Owe no man anything, but to love one another: for he, that loveth another hath fulfilled the law: Love worketh not ill to his neighbour: therefore, love is the fulfilling of the law.,*" [Romans 13:7-8,10].

PROLOGUE

Solomon speaks through his wisdom gained from experience as well, he was wise because God gave him wisdom.

Solomon, the wisest man there has ever been no human's wisdom exceeded or exceeds the wisdom of Solomon. He set in order an abundance of practical Proverbs that will help guide our life so that we are pleasing to God.

The Proverbial Woman is based on Principle. We can choose as Moses the Law Giver counseled God's people to, "*See, I have set before thee this day life and good, and death and evil; In that I command thee this day to love the Lord thy God, to walk in His ways, and to keep His commandments and His statutes and His judgments, that thou mayest live and multiply: and the Lord thy God shall bless thee in the land whither thou goest to possess it. But if thine heart turn away, so that thou wilt not hear, but shalt be drawn away, and worship other gods, and serve them; I denounce unto you this day, that ye shall surely perish, and that ye shall not prolong your days upon the land, whither thou passest over Jordan to go to possess it.*"

"*I call heaven and earth to record this day against you, that I have set before you life and death, blessing and cursing: therefore choose life, that both thou and thy seed may live: that thou mayest love the Lord thy God, and that thou mayest obey His voice, and that thou mayest cleave unto Him: for He is thy life, and the length of thy days: that thou mayest dwell in the land which the Lord swore unto thy fathers, to Abraham, to Isaac, and to Jacob, to give them*", [Deuteronomy 30:15-20].

Paul reminds us, as Moses reminded God's people then, that "*Christ hath redeemed us from the curse of the law, being made a curse for us: for it is written, cursed is everyone that hangeth on a tree: That the blessing of Abraham might come on the Gentiles through Jesus Christ; that we might receive the promise of the Spirit through faith. Brethren, I speak after the manner of men; though it be but a man's covenant, yet if it be confirmed, no man disannulleth, or addeth thereto,*" [Galatians 3:13-15].

John, the Apostle wrote, "*For God so loved the world that He gave His only Begotten Son that we through Him might live,*" [John 3:16].

"*And this is His commandment, that we should believe on the name of His Son Jesus Christ, and love one another, as He gave us commandment,*" [1 John 3:23].

The principle in this text is that God's people serve Him faithfully regardless of the generation or era which they live. He does not change; man must be willing to change, and that change is submitting ourselves to His Mighty and Divine Will for our lives and walk in a manner that is pleasing to God, "*For I am the Lord and I change not,*" [Malachi 3:6a].

The fear of God excites our love for Him through obedience.

The Scriptures gives us frequent examples, like the Proverbial Woman and the Parables spoken by Jesus, so that we will know how to be pleasing to God and what is an acceptable way of living that it will also be said of us as it was of the Proverbial Woman, "*Many daughters have done virtuously, but thou excellest them all. Favour is deceitful, and beauty is vain: but a woman that feareth the Lord, she shall be praised. Give her of the fruit of her hands; and let her own works praise her in the gates,*" [Proverbs 31:29-31].

We cannot put our confidence in ourselves, we are flesh subject to weakness and sin, nor any physical attributes we may have, God looks at the heart, which tells Him everything about us, "*I the Lord search the heart, I try the reins, even to give every man according to his ways, and according to the fruit of his doings,*" [Jeremiah 17:10].

We are striving for the goal of hearing Him say these words, which equals the words said of the Proverbial Woman; we will hear the same words. Listen to the words of our Savior, "*His Lord said unto him, Well done, good and faithful servant; thou hast been faithful over a few things, I will make thee ruler over many things: enter thou into the joy of thy Lord,*" [Matthew 25:23].

We can be assured of this fact when we are faithful to God in all things as Paul said of himself in his second letter to Timothy, "*I have fought a good fight, I have finished my course, I have kept the faith: henceforth there is laid up for me a crown of righteousness, which the Lord, the righteous judge, shall give me at that day: and not to me only, but unto all them also that love His appearing,*" [2 Timothy 4:7-8].

The Proverbial Woman is a prophetic look at our willingness to humble ourselves before God's Throne and His will for our lives. Christ left us work to do while He is away preparing our mansion for an eternity with God. He is ruling His Kingdom now. He is Priest and King advocating for us before God.

As we read Proverbs the thirty-first chapter, part one of the Proverbial Woman focuses on the wisdom a mother imparts to her son about the duties of a King and what a man's life should be and the example he is to set.

Also, the second through the fifth parts focuses on the duties of the wife and mother keeping the home while her husband/Lord/Master is away.

Those whom Christ left He can depend upon to be faithful, diligent, kind, employing the fruit of the Spirit daily.

The Proverbial Woman is also an example of a lifelong service to God. As will be mentioned in this exegesis. Throughout our lives we employ our skills as she did in performing these tasks at different intervals. These tasks outlined are not done in a day or a year, nor by every woman – every woman can utilize her skills, in service to God such as she is blessed.

Using our Spiritual magnifying glasses, every woman can see herself in this description regardless of the century, era, or time in which she lives. As well, the husbands (men) are out being the leader, doing what God has commanded.

Husbands and wives are a unit, working together for a common goal. He trusts his partner, his wife, to do what is right that God is pleased with them, and their eternal blessing will not be cut off because they wasted time, skills, and the opportunity they had to employ their skills in His service.

As well, besides them working together as the Lord directed a husband and wife are to treat each other in a manner so desired by our Savior, so their prayers will not be hindered.

Listen to what Peter the Apostle said, *"Likewise, ye wives, be in subjection to your own husbands; that, if any obey not the word, they also may without the word be won by the conversation of the wives; while they behold your chaste conversation coupled with fear. Whose adorning let it not be that outward adorning of plaiting the hair, and of wearing of gold, or of putting on of apparel; but let it be the hidden man of the heart, in that which is not corruptible, even the ornament of a meek and quiet spirit, which is in the sight of God is of great price. For after this manner in the old time the holy women also, who trusted in God, adorned themselves, being in subjection unto their own husbands: even as Sara obeyed Abraham, calling him lord: whose daughters ye are, as long as ye do well, and are not afraid with any amazement,"* [I Peter 3:1-6].

4

"Likewise, ye husbands, dwell with them according to knowledge, giving honour unto the wife, as unto the weaker vessel, and as being heirs together of the grace of life; that your prayers be not hindered. Finally, be ye all of one mind, having compassion one of another, love as brethren, be pitiful, be courteous: not rendering evil for evil, or railing for railing: but contrariwise blessing; knowing that ye are thereunto called, that ye should inherit a blessing," [I Peter 3:7-9].

James, Brother of Christ, reminds us to be dutiful to the Word, *"But be ye doers of the word, and not hearers only, deceiving your own selves. For if any be a hearer of the word, and not a doer, he is like unto a man beholding his natural face in a glass: for he beholdeth himself, and goeth his way, and straightway forgetteth what manner of man he was. But whoso looketh into the perfect law of liberty, and continueth therein, he being not a forgetful hearer; but a doer of the work, this man shall be blessed in his deed. If any man among you seems to be religious, and bridleth not his tongue, but deceiveth his own heart, this man's religion is vain. Pure religion and undefiled before God and the Father are this, to visit the fatherless and widows in their affliction, and to keep himself unspotted from the world," [James 1:22-27].*

The Book of James is also like a looking-glass, it reflects what it see: work in love (faith) purifies the heart; we are to subdue, bring our bodies in subjection (carnal lust), and obey God's commands, *"For if any be a hearer of the word, and not a doer, he is like unto a man beholding his natural face in a glass: For he beholdeth himself, and goeth his way, and straightway forgetteth what manner of man he was. But whoso looketh into the perfect law of liberty, and continueth therein, he being not a forgetful hearer, but a doer of the work, this man shall be blessed in his deed," Ibid].*

People are no different now than they were during and before Solomon's time. He noted in the first chapter of Ecclesiastes that men nor events change but are like the wind and tides of the seas which never stop moving but flows into the sea and continue back to it bed and the wind from whence it came. Listen to the wisdom of Solomon, *"One generation passeth away, and another generation cometh: but the earth abideth forever. The sun also ariseth, and the sun goeth down, and hasteth to his place where he arose. The wind goeth toward the south, and turneth about unto the north; it whirleth about continually, and the wind returneth again according to his circuits. All the rivers run into the sea; yet the sea is not full; and unto the place from whence the rivers come, thither they return again,"*

"All things are full of labour; man cannot utter it: the eye is not satisfied with seeing, nor the ear filled with hearing. The thing that hath been, it is that which shall be and that which is done is that which shall be done: and there is no new thing under

the sun. Is there anything whereof it may be said, See, this is new? it hath been already of old time, which was before us. There is no remembrance of former things; neither shall there be any remembrance of things that are to come with those that shall come after," [Ecclesiastics 1:4-11].

We like the wind and seas are never quiet in this world. We are continually seeking without ever having our appetites satisfied. Humans seeks in an unending way what they will never find because it does not exist, complete happiness and every need satisfied until we want for nothing in this life. Solomon reminds us it is a *'vexation of the spirit.'* Peace and satisfaction come only from God; there we can find peace and rest from our endless seeking on this temporal earth.

Solomon after his folly over the years said, *"I communed with mine own heart saying, "Lo, I am come to great estate, and have gotten more wisdom than all they that have been before me in Jerusalem; yea, my heart had vast experience of wisdom and knowledge," [Ecclesiastes 1:16].*

Searching for knowledge and wisdom of this world is a vexation to the mind and flesh. Constant pursuit of these wears us out and still we feel we have accomplished nothing, so we continue the pursuit. It feels like going around and around in circles of which there is no end. It was found to be vanity during Solomon's day, and it is still vanity in our day and time. The Scripture reminds us "there is nothing new under the sun.'*"The things that hath been, it is that which shall be, and that which is done is that which shall be done; and there is no new thing under the sun," [Ecclesiastes 1:9].*

> ➢ **Are the hearts and doings of men any less corrupt now than they were then?**
> ➢ **Do humans still pursue the same pots of gold at the end of that elusive rainbow?**
> ➢ **What evil or mishaps comes upon man today that is different from all the yesterday's past?**
> ➢ **Do we not fear the same things as humans did all the yesterday's past?**
> ➢ **Are not our cries, moaning, and weeping in this life about the same things as theirs were then?**

Solomon wanted us to see that the peace and happiness we want in this temporal world and temporal tent (flesh) should demand we seek out and obey the [W]ill of God for our lives. This world has only pain and heartache. Christ said, *"In this world you will have tribulation, but be of good cheer, I have overcome the world," [John 16:33b].*

This promise of true peace and happiness is in that city whose builder and maker are God, where the Tree of Life yields its fruit, and the leaves are for the healing of the nations. There the streets are paved with the gold standards of joy, peace, comfort, and the Everlasting Light coming from our Lord and Savior who provided the avenue of Salvation so that we may stop endless, empty pursuits in this life and live and serve faithfully in His Kingdom until we are called home to live in eternal bliss.

Solomon at the end of his life came to this wisdom … this wisdom is the same he counseled us to use, *"He communed with his heart,"* *[Ecclesiastes 1:16]*.

Commune is defined as meditation, reasoning with oneself.

David in the Psalms encourages us to, *"Stand in awe, and sin not; commune with your heart upon your bed, and be still,"* *[Psalms 4:4]*.

We each can speak to our hearts and say what is truth. When we are still upon our beds at night that is the perfect time to examine and search our hearts or motives.

Commune (meditation) is reflection of the day, our life, our activities, our choices, and our response to the call for obedience from our Lord and Savior Jesus Christ.

> ➢ **What good or evil was done during our waking daytime hours?**
> ➢ **Are we honest about ourselves (lives) before God?**

We admit our errors and failing as Solomon did and do not use our voices before God to try and excuse or justify our sins but use our wisdom to admit and recognize our human weaknesses and failings before the merciful God. He is our Father, knows all things and why we do the things we do.

We as parents knows why our children do the things they do and are merciful and forgiving with them when admitting their error, as we must, before God's Throne. He is our Father willing to forgive and be merciful when we repent and humble ourselves before Him.

Wisdom teaches us this as we commune daily with our hearts!

James tells us that, *"If any of you lack wisdom, let him ask of God, that giveth to all men liberally; and upbraideth not; and it shall be given to him,"* *[James 1:5]*.

Further that, "*Wisdom that is from above is first peace, then peaceable; gentle, and easy to be entreated; full of mercy and good fruit, without partiality, and without hypocrisy,*" *[James 3:17]*.

> ➤ **Is this not the very essence of what Solomon was imparting to all the hearers during his day as well as today and for all future generations as they come and go?**

God does not change no matter how long He allows the world to stand, "*I am the Lord, and I change not,*" *[Malachi 3:16a]*.

We are to learn from the whispers of the past. Paul reminded us that, "*For whatsoever things were written aforetime were written for our learning, that we through patience and comfort of the Scriptures might have hope,*" *[Romans 15:4]*.

This is wisdom that we see throughout the Scripture. Men of God penned the wisdom that we might know how to be pleasing to God. It is easy to slip into a mode of using our own wisdom (what we deem as wisdom) and script our own methods we think is pleasing to God; however, like the Apostle Paul realized on the Road to Damascus when he met Jesus, learned he could not kick against the gourd (God's will prevails), "*And when we were all fallen to the earth, I heard a voice speaking unto me, and saying in the Hebrew tongue, Saul, Saul, why persecutest thou me? it is hard for thee to kick against the pricks,*" *[Acts 26:14]*.

Jesus is in control and decides what is best for man and not man himself," "*Many plans are in a man's heart, but the purpose of the Lord will prevail,*" *[Proverbs 19:21]*.

We are also reminded that, "*A man's heart plans his way, But the Lord directs his steps,*" *[Proverbs 16:19]*.

Paul submitted to the authority of Jesus Christ rendering his weak wisdom to that of our Lord and obeyed the Gospel. We, like Paul, think we are pleasing God as he thought in his (our) self-righteousness went about destroying God's people committing them to prison and other acts against God's Commands.

As well, *[Proverbs 31]* begins with the counsel of a mother to her son the King.

Conforming to the ideology of this world for a life that is put forth as pleasing to God (man-made) is like drinking from a broken cistern.

Solomon warned about drinking from a broken cistern.

A broken cistern is a leaky vessel; it does not hold the liquid long. So, is trying to live for God as the world prescribes, it will not serve you in a positive manner in the long or short term, no more than a King's relationship with a strange woman.

In part one of the *[Thirty-first Chapter of Proverbs]*, King Lemuel's mother wanted him to understand the dangers of an association with women of the world and their ability to pull his attention away from his duties. But being faithful to the wife of his youth or the one he is married to keeps him focused and prevents error in his life, "*Drink water from your own cistern, and running water from your own well. Should your fountains be dispersed abroad, streams of water in the streets? Let them be only your own, and not for strangers with you. Let your fountain be blessed and rejoice with the wife of your youth. As a loving deer and a graceful doe, let her breasts satisfy you at all times; And always be enraptured with her love. For why should you, my son, be enraptured by an immoral woman, and be embraced in the arms of a seductress? For the ways of man are before the eyes of the Lord, and He ponders all his paths. His own iniquities entrap the wicked man, and he is caught in the cords of his sin. He shall die for lack of instruction,*" *[Proverbs 5:15-23]*.

In today's language, King Lemuel's mother did not bite her tongue when speaking with the Son of her Love, the Son of her womb as to the **"what"** questions. Being frank and to the point is where a mother needs to be at this point. He is an adult, a King, a leader, and a target for an unscrupulous woman, warns him of the traps that exists.

In Proverbs we read of the warnings of King Solomon, the Preacher, and the wisdom he imparted about a woman of questionable character, "*Drink waters out of thine own cistern, and running waters out of thine own well,*" *[Proverbs 5:15]*

And further that, "*A naughty person, a wicked man, walketh with a froward mouth he winked with his eyes, he speaketh with his feet, he teacheth with his fingers; Forwardness is in his heart, he deviseth mischief continually; he soweth discord. Therefore, shall his calamity come suddenly; suddenly shall he be broken without remedy,*" *[Proverbs 6:12-15]; [v-16-19)]*.

King Lemuel's mother need not sugarcoat, nor be vague in her warnings to her son. Mother's love their children and has the Biblical dictum to "*Train up a Child in the way they should go and when he is old will not depart from it,*" *[Proverbs 22:6]*.

Mothers continue to teach throughout their lives. Though Lemuel was King, he was her son before he was King and she has the responsibility of a parent, a mother to teacher. The Scripture does not tell the reader where the father is; therefore, the reader can ascertain from this that he (the father) at that time, for a reason not given, is not in the picture (if it is Solomon and Bathsheba we know that during Solomon's growing years David was alive, but not when he reigned as King). The Scripture does not say or verify this fact that it is Solomon and his mother. The mother here thought it of such importance that she counsels her son, even as King.

Mothers has an enormous responsibility at times even more so than the fathers. She is with that child more than the father. We see this as a fact today, there are households with the fathers absent for one reason or another; therefore, the responsibility falls to the mother.

It is apparent here that King Lemuel and his mother had a strong bond, which is a wonderful relationship for a mother and son. He respects her and is wise enough to listen to his mother's wise counsel.

A mother looks at any issue from a unique perspective, she considers all the angles and contributing factors, then come to a wise conclusion after meditation and prayer. The analogy of standing outside looking in is true. We cannot see what is around us, because we are usually too close to the situation. Women see life and situations from a more academic (hypothetical) viewpoint than a man regardless of what century or age in which they live or the culture that exists.

Regardless of the period in which humans live, wine, strong drink, and women with ultra-motives, exists; the Scripture speaks of both more than once. The Scripture reminds us of women of questionable character like (Jezebel) or a person with the [spirit] [character] she has in the examples in both Old Testament and New Testament.

Evil can influence if it is presented with words that drip like honey from its comb. Sweet words sound good to the ear. By nature, humans want love, sweetness, kind words, humans like attention, and Kings are no different. The offer of pleasure to humans is hard to resist. So, it is with a woman whose lips drip with words like the sweetness of a honeycomb is hard to resist. This is the point that King Lemuel's mother wanted him to remember and consider this lesson when this type of temptation is put before him, or he cast a wandering eye upon a beautiful female.

Drinking water from your own cistern (faithful to your wife) is pleasing to God and prevents a King from allowing his focus to be taken away from his duties.

Drinking water from a broken vessel is drinking from a leaky container. Just as fast as you put water into a pitcher that has a crack; it will slowly, on a continuous basis, trickle out. A strange woman's words are not true, nor are their motives pure, the only thing their honeycomb sweet words will do is destroy. Think about how sweet honey is; it is known as the sweetest substance on earth. When honey is used it must be sparingly, if is consumed in excess will or can make you sick.

The overuse of honey will, at a certain point in consumption, become bitter. The sweetness is gone, and it causes an unpleasant taste in your mouth. An excessive number of spoonsfuls will ruin a cup of tea. This is the point King Lemuel's mother was impressing upon his mind. Those sweet words of a strange woman are delectable, sounds good, but they become a trap. And once trapped in the long arms of their sweetness they are reluctant to let go, those sweet words then become bitter. It is usually too late at this stage; ruin has set in unnoticed.

> ➢ **How do one bounce back?**

This is a puzzling question to answer for a King or leader who has been taken in by a strange woman's sweet words and wily ways; corruption sets in at that point it is hard to bounce back, and it then effects his every action and his very decision making-abilities. Samson, as mentioned later in the text, was so enamored with Delilah, he lost sight spiritually and physically forgetting himself revealed the source of his strength (his hair).

An Angel promised Manoah wife, *"You will become pregnant and have a son whose head is never to be touched by a razor because the boy is to be a Nazirite, dedicated to God from the womb. He will take the lead in delivering Israel from the hands of the Philistines," [Judges 3:15].*

He was dedicated to the service of God to use for His purpose. He was chosen to be the deliver of Israel from the hands of their enemy. We, like Samson, can forget ourselves as well. We cannot say that it will not happen to me, all are flesh and the flesh is weak. God gave Samson the victorious strength he had but he allowed his focus to be taken by the sweet pleas of Delilah blinding him; can you not hear her and that deadly declarative statement? **"If you love me, you will tell me the secret of your strength!"**

Sweet words that dripped like honey from a comb!

He fell into the pit she dug for him, of lust and desire.

Samson did not fall at once, there were allurements used by Delilah leading up to the point he revealed to her the source of his strength. She applies the pressure with temptations (moveable, ever changing) wore his resistance down with her female wiles.

We can see Satan's fingerprints all over this. Let us listen to what Peter and Paul says to Christians because we are aware of the processes Satan uses to destroy us with those sneak attacks. We are to, *"Be sober, be vigilant; because your adversary the devil, as a roaring lion, walketh about, seeking whom he may devour,"* *[I Peter 5:8]* and Scripture warns children to *"Obey their father and mother, which is the first commandment of promise,"* *[Ephesians 6:2].*

Samson forgot the teaching of his mother and went after a woman of the same people from whom he was delivering Israel. He paid a high price for his error and disobedience to the will of God for his life, in the end, his sight gone, died with all the Philistines in the colosseum that day.

Satan used Samson's lust for Delilah against him. Satan has always hated God; he still hates God.

Also, Samson's wife, a Philistine woman from Timnah, betrayed him with the answer to the riddle after three days the Philistines still could not figure it out, *"And he said unto them, Out of the eater came forth meat, and out of the strong came forth sweetness. And they could not in three days expound the riddle,"* *[Judges 14:14].*

They encouraged his wife to entice him to give them the answer to the riddle with threats of death to she and her household, *[Judges 14:15]*

"So, Samson's wife went to him in tears and said, "You don't love me! You just hate me! You told my friends a riddle and didn't tell me what it means!"

He said, *"Look, I haven't even told my father and mother. Why should I tell you?" She cried about it for the whole seven days of the feast. But on the seventh day he told her what the riddle meant, for she nagged him so about it. Then she told the Philistines,"[Judges 14:16–17].*

Satan is our adversary as he was King Lemuel's, Samson, David the King, or any King/leader who served God. Life and evil on this earth are what every human must deal with. Evil is here, Satan is the instigator of it, and he targets God's people with the intent to destroy. Satan uses stacking in his deceptive methods to snare man. He adds but never subtracts the attractive things of this world that is destructive to the soul. The deviousness of a wicked woman is only one of the numerous tools he uses. King Lemuel's mother reminds him they (strange women) will ruin you; they do not assist you, not in a positive manner.

Where there is a deceptive female there is always liquor; it gives a trancing effect to the mind. Wine and strong drink in this case, like a wicked woman with honeycomb sweet words, that combination can and will bring ruin. Paul tells us to, *"Touch not, taste not, handle not," [Colossians 2:21].*

We are saved from the [rudiments] of this world through Christ.

> ➤ **Why dabble in the pleasures of the world again once we are washed through Baptism with the Blood of Christ and are no longer tainted with it amusements?**

The gratifications and things of the world are deep pits for God's people.

> ➤ **I always think of how pleasing chocolate is, white, dark, or caramel; who does not like chocolate?**

Chocolate is enjoyable when eating it; but has a negative effect eventually if you, overtime, over-indulge in it. The delightful taste that it gives is what we as humans desire without considering the end results.

Servants of sin has several masters; the chief among these are lust, pride, and covetousness; each has lots of children. Lust drives them in numerous directions, pride carries them down dead-end paths, and covetousness pilots them headlong to destruction.

The Scripture teaches us that we can trust God. It is using wisdom when we put our trust in God and not humans. Solomon reminds that, *"Trust in the Lord with all thine heart; and lean not unto thine own understanding. In all thy ways acknowledge [Him], and [He] shall direct thy paths," [Proverbs 5:5-6].*

The things that God hates, we as Christians must hate those things as well and avoid them, this also applies to a King and the words of a strange woman because, *"Her ways are moveable that thou canst not know them,"* *[Proverbs 5:6b].*

What great a matter does a little fire kindle. Becoming friendly with people who are out of the "way" is a danger; it looks innocent at the beginning, but later it grows into shame and embarrassment, which incurs God's wrath. We should avoid sin and all its approaches, traps, and attractiveness.

This is an indication of the score of strategies used by a strange woman; she never uses the same tactics, critiquing them to that man, they are always changing as time goes on as the strategies are successful. We are reminded in Scripture of these actions of a person with this type of character and them indulging in the delights of the world and the lust thereof.

Job reminds us in this manner, *"How much more abominable and filthy is man, which drinketh iniquity like water?" [Job 15:15].*

When subjugated by her (strange woman); it is like taking fire to your chest; fire is damaging, it destroys, and burns all that is in its wake; however, when we follow God's commandments for our lives is acting on wisdom. Listen at the counsel of the Preacher, *"For the commandment is a lamp; and the law is light; and reproofs of instruction are the ways of life: To keep thee from the evil woman, from the flattery of the tongue of a strange woman. Lust not after her beauty in thine heart; neither let her take thee with her eyelids. For by means of a whorish woman a man is brought to a piece of bread: and the adulteress will hunt for the precious life. Can a man take fire in his bosom, and his clothes not be burned? Can one go upon hot coals, and his feet not be burned? So, he that goeth into his neighbor's wife; whosoever toucheth her shall not be innocent," [Proverbs 6:24-29].*

The strange and adulterous woman lives in a chronic way according to her lust, there is no righteousness in her thoughts nor actions there is only her selfishness need to satisfy the lust that has overcome her being, mind, body, soul, and spirit. King Lemuel's Mother knew this and cautioned the King of the vileness of a person with these kinds of desires in her heart and mind.

Satan uses this type of strategy; humans are at a disadvantage to know how he will come at us. Paul reminds us we need the whole armor of Christ from head to foot to protect us from the darts that he aims at us. We get our strength to fight against Satan from God; we cannot fight alone an enemy we cannot see. He is the ruler of the darkness of this world.

Listen to Paul's counsel, *"Finally, my brethren, be strong in the Lord, and in the power of His might. Put on the whole armor of God, that ye may be able to stand against the wiles of the devil. For we wrestle not against flesh and blood, but against principalities, against powers, against the rulers of the darkness of this world, against spiritual wickedness in high places. Wherefore take unto you the whole armor of God, that ye may be able to withstand in the evil day, and having done all, to stand,"* [Ephesians 6:10-13; 14-20].

As Proverbs reminds us, the wiles and wickedness of Satan are, *"moveable, thou canst not know it"* indicates the wily ways – moveable is never permanent in nature or implementation.

Satan uses many rivulets and tributaries of human desires to feed into the oceans of sin engulfing the lives of man. As the centuries goes on, his stacking of attractive sins increases. The more humans' desires increase so does Satan's increase of the sins. The Scripture tells us that God said before he destroyed all living things on land in the air that the imagination and thoughts of the heart of man then were evil continually, *"And God saw that the wickedness of man was great in the earth, and that every imagination of the thoughts of his heart was only evil continually. And it repented the Lord that [He] had made man on the earth, and it grieved [Him] at [His] heart. And the Lord said, "[I] will destroy man whom [I] have created from the face of the earth; both man, and beast, and the creeping thing, and the fowls of the air; for it repenteth [Me] that [I] have made them,"* [Genesis 6:5-7].

> ➢ **Have the thoughts and imaginations of the hearts of man changed?**
> ➢ **Are they still evil continually?**

Satan provides the avenues of sins of which man indulges and then accuses man before the throne of God of those same sins. He still speaks with the same forked tongue now as he did in the Garden of Eden.

The Proverbial Woman as can be ascertained from the Scripture, did not travel down any of the avenues of sin that he proposed. She, like we, I am sure, were tempted in all ways, but won the battle, as we can and will if we keep the faith, stay on the course, stay faithful, and lastly remember what Paul the Apostle said about people of God when they are being tempted, *"There is no temptation taken you, but such as is common to man, but God is faithful who will not suffer you to be tempted above what ye are able; but will with the temptation also make a way to escape; that you may be able to bear it,"* [I Corinthians 10:13].

Satan offers only a thin veneer of what is right but does not go far enough for it to be right. He, as we know from Scripture, used the Scripture, taking it out of context while our Savior was in the wilderness. He takes it out of context and makes it sound good, which if one has a willing ear, he will lead you down the path to the only end he can offer, destruction and eternal separation from God.

The wickedness of a strange woman is also a by-product of our chief adversary.

She will use whatever works on the victim she is targeting. When taken in by the delights and darlings of her pleasures along with strong drink is a deep narrow pit. The Scripture reminds us that she pursues (hunts), *"Remove thy way far from her; come not nigh the door of her house; Lest thou give thine honour unto others, and thy years unto the cruel: lest strangers be filled with thy wealth; and thy labors be in the house of a stranger; And thou mourn at the last, when thy flesh and thy body are consumed," [Proverbs 5:8-11].*

We cannot see into the dark minds of anyone who indulges in these types of strategies. Solomon warned us in his wisdom the danger of "moveable" ways. He had experienced all of this as we read in Ecclesiastics. The entire book focuses on things that are pursued that are vain, *"Vanities of Vanities, all is Vanity," [Ecclesiastes 1:2].*

We are to be, therefore, wise enough, to follow the path that God desires for our lives and not chase after the things of the world that causes our focus to be drawn away in other directions. Christ tells us, *"Seek ye first the Kingdom of Heaven and Its righteousness and all of these things will be added unto you," [Matthew 6:33].*

> ➤ **What things?**

God provides all that we need in life, if we are faithful and trust him and not run after the shadowy and fading vanities that this world has to offer.

The attractive excess of this world only lasts a moment in time before ruin for an eternity or the ruination of a King's Kingdom takes place. Licentiousness, Solomon warned, fleshly lust is not of God. King Lemuel's Mother is aware of the dangers of this evil sin and the surety of it, that it would destroy him and his kingdom.

Sin of any nature has these characteristics and is more than capable of destroying life; and its end is death; a horrible pit for an eternity if it is not shunned and avoided. Do not desire her – her lips are sweet is what Solomon's is saying, also it can be compared to a woman of evil and wicked intentions. Just as lust can overtake a King it can overtake a female as well.

16

How bitter the fruit of it to the spiritual taste!

The taste (pleasure) of those fleshly desires might be enjoyable in the beginning, but over time, as one gratifies (fills) themselves with its pleasing taste, it become bitter for the soul, "*My son, keep my words, and lay up my commandments with thee. Keep my commandments, and live; and my law as the apple of thine eye. Bind them upon thy fingers, write them upon the table of thine heart. Say unto wisdom, thou art my sister; and call understanding thy kinswoman: That they may keep thee from the strange woman, from the stranger which flattereth with her words. For at the window of my house I looked through my casement, and beheld among the simple ones, I discerned among the youths, a young man void of understanding, passing through the street near her corner; and he went the way to her house.*

"*In the twilight, in the evening, in the black and dark night: And behold, there met him a woman with the attire of a harlot, and subtil of heart. (She is loud and stubborn; her feet abide not in her house: Now is she without, now in the streets, and lieth in wait at every corner.) So, she caught him, and kissed him, and with an impudent face said unto him, I have peace offerings with me; this day have I payed my vows. Therefore, came I forth to meet thee, diligently to seek thy face, and I have found thee. I have decked my bed with coverings of tapestry, with carved works, with fine linen of Egypt. I have perfumed my bed with myrrh, aloes, and cinnamon. Come, let us take our fill of love until the morning: let us solace ourselves with loves,*" [Proverbs 7:1-18].

"*She lieth in wait at every corner,*" expresses the danger of youthful lust.

King Lemuel was subject to this like any other young man. "*She lieth in wait at every corner*" expresses that the sin of lust can happen; it is unavoidable in this world, waiting to trap you, but we can choose not to partake is why King Lemuel's mother warned him as Solomon the Preacher warns us – consider it is the same for young women as it is for young men. It, (lust), has no respect of person; we are all susceptible to it.

Solomon said wisdom is needed but surrounding that wisdom is also a need for a clear understanding, no one is exempt. As King Lemuel's mother continued to counsel and teach, so must we instruct our sons as well as daughters, and grandchildren.

This counsel can influence their lives enormously as well the impact can bring about positive and lasting change – counseling is for correction and reproof. Paul reminds us that is what the Word of God does for our lives if we are willing to adhere to its wisdom, *"All Scripture is given by inspiration of God, and is profitable for doctrine, for reproof, for correction, for instruction in righteousness," [2 Timothy 3:16-17].*

It is a blessing to have such a caring and understanding mother, as King Lemuel did, who can guide and help his avoiding the steps that leads into a pit of darkness, become displeasing in the sight of God, and cause the downfall of his reign.

The Parables in Proverbs are instructive and enriches our lives so that we might be pleasing to God.

There are so many parables that uses the female gender to express their point.

King Lemuel's mother did not share her knowledge and experience with him in a parroting manner (telling him do not do the same as any Biblical figure who were in a leadership or King over a Kingdom). She spoke to him as a mother would a son who she bought up at her knee distinguishing for him the difference between right and wrong and what pleased and displeased the God of Heaven. She wanted him to be knowledgeable and learned in issues of life that he might become self-sufficent in his duties as King.

The saying we know in our time, *"all eyes are on you"* is applicable here. All eyes were on the King at that moment because he was the leader, and final decisions, laws, and rules were made or approved by the King.

King Lemuel's mother had raised him in a respectful manner. She was able to give him sound advice on which he could depend. He was familiar with her sound advice, strong hand in his life, and now she could yet advise him in the manner that a man should conduct himself before he becomes King not after he become King and has fallen prey to the wiles of a strange woman.

(We are to arm ourselves with the knowledge of what pleases God just as King Lemuel's mother armed him so when he (or we) meets temptation on the paths of life he (we) know how to resist it or avoid it all together, realizing yet again, we cannot resist temptation alone; we need the help of the only one who can help us, Our God).

At that point there had been a transfer of knowledge and King Lemuel could stand on his own because he was mature. But warnings of traps or deep pits was still necessary because he is a target simply because he is the King.

People like bling in any age; a King was certainly bling to a strange woman.

King Lemuel did not need training wheels anymore he needed to know how to use the road map and where the speed traps are and the stop signs that are not visible sometimes until he is right up on them and stopping in time becomes difficult.

Losing the greater for the less is always tragic.

Think of losing the greater for the less Samson did, for a while; he forgot who he is … a child of God, a servant, a leader, a judge, a deliverer who was chosen by God for service before his birth.

King Lemuel's mother wanted him to remain faithful, at the duties of which he was appointed and not stray off the given path and obligation as the King and leader of his people, but remain focused … Learning to do well is a must to be pleasing to God and in the duties that He so appoints us," *Learn to do well; seek judgment, relieve the oppressed, judge the fatherless, plead for the widow,"* [Isaiah 1:17].

Micah, the Prophet, further reminds us, as it was then so it is now, *"He hath shewed thee, O man, what is good; and what doth the Lord require of thee, but to do justly, and to love mercy, and to walk humbly with thy God?"* [Micah 6:8].

King Lemuel's mother wanted him to focus on his responsibilities and the burdens of a King. He has so much to attend giving his time and strength to a strange woman is a waste of his time and power.

It is the same today with our sense of duty to God as we will see further in the text and the description of a woman and her household task. The everyday care and concern she has of making sure all things and everyone are taken care of, forgetting nothing, not even the trivial things in life that falls under her umbrella of responsibilities, so does insignificant things fall under the King. It is often, in life, it is the lack of attention to the trivial matters that can be more destructive, simply because we are not walking circumspectly or remaining cognizant of our surroundings and the actions and words of people with whom we come in contact.

Listen at the wisdom of a wise King.

Solomon took time to solve the question of the two women and one dead child and one live child. He could have easily pushed this grave situation aside as unimportant to his reign; he did not, but took the responsibility of solving the problem for that mother standing there with her heart being torn out, because she thought she would lose her child to another woman with evil intents; they were prostitutes, but also important to him because they were humans and deserved to have justice; as well, they were also part of the people of his vast kingdom.

He listened, discerned, and judged between right and wrong between these two women and through his wisdom showed who the mother of the live child was because she was willing for that child to live opposed to the other woman who said do not allow the child to live. Solomon said, *"Divide the child give one half to one and one half to the other."* The mother cried out in pain let her have the child I would rather it live, *"The preparations of the heart in man, and the answer of the tongue, is from the Lord. All the ways of a man are clean in his own eyes; but the Lord weigheth the spirits,"* [Proverbs 16:1-2].

A perfect display of the wisdom of a King to know the truth and that he stands on what is right and against what is wrong, *"A just weight and balance are the Lord's: all the weights of the bag are His work,"* [Proverbs 16:11].

Truth should not be a respecter of a person, nor should be righteous judgment.

God requires a scale of balance. The people of God are required to be honest in their relationships with their fellowman and with God. We cannot have a pleasing relationship with God nor man if we are not honest…honesty establishes a King's reign one that is pleasing before the God of Heaven.

He, Solomon, in this instant, was both King and Judge. Therefore, his judgment must be fair and his mind clear to make those judgments not clouded with wine, strong drink, or thoughts of a strange woman could all be a distraction from his responsibilities to the people who are in his Kingdom.

A strange woman's two cousins' intent and betrayal are her [constant] companions. Their kisses are as deadly as the one that betrayed Christ.

Judas' kiss betrayed Jesus, *"Now he that betrayed Him gave them a sign, saying, Whomsoever I shall kiss, that same is He: hold Him fast. And forthwith he came to Jesus, and said, Hail, Master; and kissed Him. And Jesus said unto him, friend, wherefore art thou come? Then came they, and laid hands-on Jesus, and took Him,"* [Matthew 26:48-50].

When I read of the sweet lips of strange women dripping like a honeycomb and the kiss of Judas, they accomplish the same end [*Proverbs 5, Ibid*].

A kiss that supposes to be an act of friendship, as well it was an act of the greatest betrayal that has ever existed especially when our Savior was betrayed by one of his own with a kiss.

Just as the kiss of the betrayal was foretold in Scripture a mother tells her son that the lips of strange women can betray a King as well. Judas betrayed Christ with his lips, unspoken betrayal. The strange woman act of betrayal is spoken and unspoken with her lips. A kiss can be as sweet as honey which is an analogy used today – just as honey has hidden bitterness so her honey laced words and kisses can become bitterness to a King.

King Lemuel's mother knew this, who better can tell their son about the wiles of strange women … women know the capabilities of other women. A woman, as said before, looks at any situation entirely different than a male will when she notices a male, king, or leader is approached by an unscrupulous female with honey laced bitterness and destruction dripping from her lips.

A woman can immediately recognize an unscrupulous woman the way she carries herself; the look in her eyes; the greedy smile; and the annoying presence that she forces upon the environment.

> - **A woman's instantly ask, 'why is she being so sweet?'**
> - **What is she up to?**
> - **She ends with the declarative statement, "No woman is honey sweet all the time that is just not our nature!"**

Disrupt the King and the Kingdom is weak because the leader has been compromised, his power is threatened as well. King Lemuel's mother knew all of this and counseled her son in a preventative manner. His mother had seen more years of life than he and could warn him. Kings has a certain conduct and reputation to maintain, and his behavior or status cannot be tainted or marred by even a moment of indiscretion.

When experience is speaking wisdom is displayed. We are wise when we sit and listen to the "what" questions as King Lemuel did when his mother spoke to him.

Being in a state of bestir (awakeness) is wise …mentally awareness that these snares in life needs avoiding. Falling into the deep pits of temptation where no waters of life flow only darkness, sorrow, and pains come-to-pass, is a recipe for destruction, whether it be a King over a Kingdom or a woman in charge of her household.

We read of the relationship of King Lemuel and his mother. It is thought that the King here and his mother could be Solomon and Bathsheba as mentioned before; however, Scripture does not confirm this. There is no other description of a King Lemuel in Scripture as it is of other Kings who reigned. We know of Bathsheba. She was married to David the King and had the chance to take advantage of the wisdom of King David. She paid a price for her wisdom because of her relationship with King David, and the act that was displeasing to the God of Heaven which resulted in the loss of her first child.

There is no evidence that this is Bathsheba and Solomon, but it [could be] makes sense. A mother instructing the son of her womb, one whom she loved so much, is precious to her, knew he had an overwhelming task of being just the Son of King David, expectations were high and the kingdom of which he had rule, was vast.

Also, she wanted to ensure that Solomon's position was secure before David died. She reminded him of his promise to her. One of David's other sons announced himself as King even before King David died.

There was none finer raised than Solomon. His youth paints of picture of a resolute and obedient son. We also see a portrait of a devoted mother who loved her son enough to teach him patiently and meticulously from her knowledge and wisdom.

This can be a portrait of faithful women or can be the portrait of a mother who serves God and wants her son to walk the same path guided by the wisdom she imparts.

Leaving for a moment the portrait she paints for a wise son, let us concentrate on mothers and children period. The Book of Proverbs exemplifies the wisdom of Solomon. That wisdom comes from God. The mother speaking here is also wise through the blessings of God.

Wisdom does not live in conceit. A wise king concentrates on his subjects and not the fact that he has the privilege to do whatsoever his heart desires.

Wisdom does heed the fact that absolute power can corrupt absolutely.

When the use of wisdom is absent in the daily life of a king/leader, regardless of who they are or which century they live, allows deceit to drive their decisions and actions instead of wisdom, shows their focus is off the duties required of the king/leader are on himself and the pleasures of this world, "*Love not the world, neither the things that are in the world. If any man loves the world, the love of the Father is not in him. For all that is in the world, the lust of the flesh, and the lust of the eyes, and the pride of life, is not of the Father, but is of the world. And the world passeth away, and the lust thereof: but he that doeth the will of God abideth forever,*" [I John 2:15-17].

Satan's seduction of God's people is an ongoing factor.

From the beginning of time (creation of man) Satan, beginning with Eve, launched his conquest of destruction and campaign of ruin against God and His people and will continue until this earth is no more and the final judgment takes place. He, unfortunately, is a master at drawing people in, making right seem wrong and wrong seem right. He is the virtuoso of deception is why remaining vigilant and mindful each minute of the day is crucial. "He attacks when you least expect" is a thought, but one that a Christian is well-aware of.

Scripture warns us of the wiles of Satan.

God's people cannot take a fetal position with Satan. Sin is like a cloud; it separates man from the Light of God. We cannot see God in the face of sin and disobedience which blocks the light of Salvation as the clouds does the sun.

Satan was the architect and orchestrator of "mayhem" during the time the Proverbial Woman's lived, as he is now. He is the author of sin and disobedience; he does not change but get increasingly worse, opening the storehouses, of all his sinful pleasures, for man to enjoy, as times winds down.

The people of God, if they do not remain vigilant, will suffer spiritual atrocities at the hands of Satan. He is the arch enemy of God's people. His only goal is to destroy and take to eternal destruction all that he can who falls prey to his allurements; he has no hope of peace; he lost that hope when he presumed to be more powerful than the Creator of all things, including him, "*Let every soul be subject unto the higher powers. For there is no power but of God: the powers that be are ordained of God,*" [Romans 13:1].

We can look through the lens of history in today's dispensation of time and discern and understand that the wisdom of Solomon and the example of the Proverbial Woman applies to us in every way when we are mothers, wives, and responsible for the duties of our households.

A good wife stands out like a Lily among thorns, just the Bride of Christ, the Church, shines like the brilliance of the north star in a shadowy world.

A good wife is refreshing like a spring day, which brings blessings in the life of her husband, children, maidens, servants, and the overall community.

The picture of the Bride of Christ, His Church, which is holy, spotless, and without blemish, by the Gift of the Blood of Christ, is vividly described with the beauty of a bride that is relatable.

The only way to heaven is through the training ground on earth we [must] travel through the wilderness of this world there is no other way provided for man to inherit heaven.

Christ came and showed us how to make the journey successfully through all the trials and tribulations on the pathways in the wilderness of the world. The children of Israel traveled through the wilds on their way to the promise land symbolically used here as an example; so, must we travel through the "back of beyond" during our journey on the way to the eternal promised land.

This example is used in a symbolistic manner of the trials and resistance we sometimes meet on our journey. The thirst that our soul has for peace, the hunger for comfort of the spirit, the need for rest from our labor: only Christ can provide those things. He is our rock, the life-giving stream, our manna, and our land flowing with milk and honey, "*Come to Me all ye that labour and are heavy laden, and I will give you rest. Take My yoke upon you and learn of Me; for I am meek and lowly in heart and ye shall find rest your souls, for My yoke is easy and My burden is light,*" [Matthew 11:28-30].

Sometimes life kills the dreams we have due to circumstances and happenstances, but this life cannot kill our hope through faith in the promises of our Lord and Savior of a better and more enduring country, "*Now faith is the substance of things hoped for and the evidence of things not seen,*" [Hebrews 11:1].

Earth is the only training ground. If we are not obedient to Christ here, we will not have peace in eternity. Christ is coming back for His Bride, The Kingdom of which He is reigning King.

We must be in the Kingdom under His rule now. The Proverbial Woman knew the importance of the future benefits of obeying and being a faithful servant, she as the Hebrew writer said of Abraham *"For he looked for a city which hath foundations, whose builder and maker is God,"* [Hebrews 11:10].

The foundations of this world are shaky at best. All things man-made are perishable with the using. God created the universe and all things therein; including the earth, but we keep in mind that Satan is the god of this world. Nothing he has, promises, or gives, has any lasting value to the soul in eternity, nor the physical life here, *"In whom the god of this world hath blinded the minds of them which believe not, lest the light of the glorious Gospel of Christ, who is the image of God, should shine unto them,"* [2 Corinthians 4:4].

"Blessed is everyone that feareth the Lord; that walketh in His ways. For thou shalt eat the labour of thine hands: happy shalt thou be, and it shall be well with thee. Thy wife shall be as a fruitful vine by the sides of thine house: thy children like olive plants round about thy table. Behold, that thus shall the man be blessed that feareth the Lord. The Lord shall bless thee out of Zion: and thou shalt see the good of Jerusalem all the days of thy life. Yea, thou shalt see thy children's children, and peace upon Israel," [Psalms 128:1-6].

Mold-fitting is a dangerous place to live in this world.

We cannot pander to the demands that society pushes us to succumb to its idea of what a woman looks like. Mold-fitting according to society has no wisdom attached to it. Molds change in size, in scope, and in appearance. It is like marketing; it fits the needs of the product at that time to get it pushed through the market. When that strategy has garnered as much profitability as possible for that period, it changes.

Molds, like fashions, changes every season and that season is dependent upon where one is in the world at that time or the culture into which they are assimilating. We are familiar with how quickly change happens, which demands a hither and yond viewpoint. Lest we forget who the orchestrator of the constant change in the world is and the hither and yond way he positions the evil he perpetrates among humans; he is the god of this world; therefore, his entire operation is flawed and based on a lie.

In this light, the example of the Proverbial Woman is consistent, unwavering, resolute, and focused. She stays on track with her duties. The five areas of the wisdom of King Lemuel's Mother are shown in Scripture. Her wisdom shines as she speaks with her son. She does not allow the world and Satan in his efforts to destroy God's people to place her in the mold (s) he has proposed.

Consistency in His commands for our lives are what is pleasing to God.

God does not change, nor does His commands change given us in Scripture – Scripture is the Living Word of God because God is the eternal living, all-seeing, all-knowing, and the ever-present Sovereign.

We walk by God's commands, not rules of the world or what is done by the majority. Taking a stand or standing on the Word of God is difficult in the world filled with opposition borne from our chief adversary, but if we expect to inherit Eternity with Christ must live faithfully regardless of how the world changes or the molds of society comes and goes.

The [Graces] of the Spirit of God are ornaments to His people.

Righteousness is like fine linen.

Our lives must be pure before God, not perfect, but serve Him in Spirit and in truth. Fine Linen is described as clean, white, an indication of purity. The Priest wore Linen before God – our righteousness is like the fine linen that the Proverbial Woman made garments of denoting purity of the Church, the Bride of Christ.

Hear what John the Apostle wrote when he spoke with the angel, *"Let us be glad and rejoice, and give honor to Him: for the marriage of the Lamb is come, and His wife hath made herself ready. And to her was granted that she should be arrayed in fine Linen, clean, and white, for the Linen is the righteousness of Saints. And he saith unto me write, "Blessed are they which are called unto the marriage supper of the Lamb." And he saith unto me, "These are the true saying of God," and I fell at his feet and worshiped him, "He said unto me, see thou do it not: I am they fellow servant, and of thy brethren that have the testimony of Jesus: Worship God: for the testimony of Jesus is the Spirit of Prophecy."*

John the Apostle's then describes the omnipotent, omnipresence, and omniscience Lord and Savior, *"Then I saw heaven opened and behold a white horse; and He that sat upon him was called Faithful and True, and in righteousness He hath judge and made war. His eyes were as a flame of fire, and on His head were many* crowns; and He had a name written, that no man knew, but He Himself. And He was clothed with a vesture dripped in blood: and His name is called the Word of God. And the armies which were in heaven follow Him upon white horses, clothed in fine linen, white and clean," [Revelations 19:7-14].

As God told Abraham to walk through the land, we are to do so here and not think it is a final place or fixed here for an eternity; but look for a better country whose foundation, builder, and maker is God where those who remain faithful will be clothed with fine linen, pure, white, and clean.

The Proverbial Woman thought the more and better enduring substance of Heaven worthy of her diligence, faith, faithfulness, and working in God's service that she would inherit the everlasting crown for an eternity.

Peter the Apostle reminds us that we are sojourners, not permanent residents of this earth, it should be done in reverence and fear, "And if ye call on the Father, Who without respect of persons judgeth according to every man's work, pass the time of your sojourning here in fear," [I Peter 1:17].

As well James, the Lord's Brother wrote as guided by the Holy Spirit, "Whereas ye know not what shall be on the morrow. For what is your life? It is even a vapour, that appeareth for a little time, and then vanisheth away," [James 4:14].

Paul assures us that Scripture is the Word of God and, "All scripture is given by inspiration of God, and is profitable for doctrine, for reproof, for correction, for instruction in righteousness: that the man of God may be perfect, thoroughly furnished unto all good works," [2 Timothy 3:16-17].

Peter further reminds us that Scripture did not originate from man, through written by men as they were guided by the Holy Spirit and wisdom dictates that we do well when we heed the Word, "We have also a more sure word of prophecy; whereunto ye do well that ye take heed, as unto a light that shineth in a dark place, until the day dawn, and the day star arise in your hearts. Knowing this first, that no prophecy of the scripture is of any private interpretation. For the prophecy came not in old time by the will of man: but holy men of God spake as they were moved by the Holy Ghost," [2 Peter 1:19-21].

The Proverbial Woman gives the example for others to know how to be obedient; how to live a serious life; she taught the essence of self-denial; the contempt for the ways of the world; and the benefits of her focus on God and eternity.

A waste of time and not serving God in the manner that is commanded in any era is not wise. Christ when speaking with the Pharisee spoke to them of bringing fruit to God through their works, *"And now also the axe is laid unto the root of the trees: therefore, every tree which bringeth not forth good fruit is hewn down, and cast into the fire,"* [Matthew 3:10].

Outward services without inward change are vanity and deceptive to one's mind. It is a tool of Satan.

Satan only offers misery. Sin is a sickness, a destructive disease, and it is a torment to the Soul.

We have examples of those who, like the Proverbial Woman, was pleasing to God and her fruit (work) is written in Scripture that we might know and understand the importance of the duties of a wife, mother, neighbor, servant, merchant, and employer in her days as it is now. Paul expresses it this way in our race to eternity, *"Wherefore seeing we also are compassed about with so great a cloud of witnesses, let us lay aside every weight, and the sin which doth so easily beset us, and let us run with patience the race that is set before us, looking unto Jesus the author and finisher of our faith, who for the joy that was set before him endured the cross, despising the shame, and is set down at the right hand of the Throne of God,"* [Hebrews 12:1-2].

God uses the foolish (simple) things of the world to confound the wise. As well, the simplicity of the lessons in the Proverbial Woman is the Wisdom of God. We are wise to heed the day-to-day duties that the Proverbial Woman did and never allowing her mind to be the playground for the devil nor her hands idle so he could use them to do evil, nor did she think these responsibilities beneath her, but with humility and obedience performed them each with diligence, love, care, and in a timely manner. Scripture tells us, *"But God hath chosen the foolish things of the world to confound the wise; and God hath chosen the weak things of the world to confound the things which are mighty; And base things of the world, and things which are despised, hath God chosen, yea, and things which are not, to bring to nought things that are: That no flesh should glory in His presence,"* [I Corinthians 1:27-29].

The mother of King Lemuel, in the Proverbs 31 text, gave a vivid description of two types of women who are a danger to a King that he needs to be aware of; as well in her narrative, the qualities to look for in a woman who would make a faithful and godly wife. She added the color and context in painting the portrait of both. She gave explicit reasons why choosing one and not the other or avoiding one and clinging to the other is either unwise or wise.

The strange or adulterous woman wraps her evil intent and dishonesty in smiles, body language, and in her words that drips with sweetness like honey from a comb, as did Delilah's words, actions, and pretense of care, in her evil objective in the betrayal of Samson.

King Lemuel's mother described the types of evil perpetrated by a strange or an adulterous woman in a manner that is in-depth in the warnings to her son.

As well, she painted on a different canvas a portrait of the godly woman and the attributes and characteristics that would be a benefit and a feature in his life, his family's life, and the community; additionally, it gives women today and ones in future generations, a clear and comprehensive narrative of a woman's life, who will have the approval of the God of all creation, who lives a godly life before God and can inherit eternity.

A King who conducts himself in a righteous manner, do not allow his reputation to be tainted by association with strange or adulterous women, is not given to strong drink, which defiles the heart and mind, fair in judgment, speaking for the poor and those who are helpless, staying focused on his duties as a leader and protector of his people, and one who has a virtuous wife is far richer than all the gold of his kingdom, because he is pleasing to God.

INTRODUCTION

The Proverbial Woman, [*Chapter 31*], of The Book of Proverbs is divided into five areas: Judging Righteously; The Price of the Virtuous Woman; The Virtuous Woman cares for her family; The Virtuous Woman helps the needy; and The Virtuous Woman speaks Wisdom.

The book of Daniel gives a thought-provoking example of a King (Nebuchadnezzar) coming to the full understanding, after numerous trails, a loss of his kingdom, punishment for his lack of reverence before the Almighty and Sovereign God who Reigns Supreme, is the giver of all power, raises up and brings down kingdoms and men according to His Mighty Will, and not their own.

He desiring to be worshipped and other defiant acts caused his kingdom to be torn from him, he became a beast with feather and claws, eating grass as an ox until he humbled himself and learned that the God of heaven is the only God; and his kingdom was returned to him by the Only God, ruler over heaven and earth and all that dwells therein.

"And at the end of the days, I Nebuchadnezzar, lifted up mine eyes unto heaven, and mine understanding returned unto me, and I blessed the Most High, and I praised and honoured Him that liveth forever, [W]hose dominion is an everlasting dominion, and His Kingdom is from generation to generation," [Daniel 4:35].

King Lemuel's mother taught him that judging righteously is essential in life.

PART I:

JUDGING RIGHTEOUSLY
PROVERBS 31:1-9

V1: The words of King Lemuel, the prophecy that his mother taught him," [Proverbs 31:1].

Parents has the responsibility of raising their children in a manner that is approved of by God. Discipline is necessary and should not be withheld from children as they grow. A child left to himself knows not what road to take unless he is shown. The fruit of his raising will become evident, "*The rod of reproof gives wisdom; but a child left to himself bringeth his mother to shame,*" [Proverbs 29:15].

Solomon further warns that parents are to, "*Correct thy son, and he shall give thee rest; yea, he shall give delight unto thy soul,*" [Proverbs 29:17].

There is nothing worse than a child who brings shame, sorrow, and pain to a mother's heart for the lack of guidance. King Lemuel's mother knew her responsibility as a parent and went about raising her son in a manner that is approved by God.

Children are a heritage from God which is a blessing. Mothers have the greatest honor from God - He blesses her with the privilege of being a mother and having charge of a precious soul she is given to raise and nurture that child, seeking wisdom from the Heavenly Father, "*Lo children are a heritage of the Lord; and the fruit of the womb is His reward,*" [Psalms 127:3].

Moses wrote we are to teach our children on a continuous basis, "*And these only words, which I command thee this day, shall be in thine heart; and thou shalt teach them diligently unto thy children and shalt talk of them when thou sitteth in thine house, and when thou walkest by the way, and when thou lieth down, and when thou riseth up,*" [Deuteronomy 6:6-7].

V2: What, my son? and what, the son of my womb? and what, the son of my vow?" [Proverbs 31:2].

The Hebrew word for 'what' is implicit to "*Hear O Israel*" that Moses used when instructing the people of God. Listen, is an overall view of the word, 'what.' I have something important to say to you is another concept.

A mother's advice is timely and helpful, a priceless jewel. She would know that a faithful woman suited for her son would need to be virtuous. She gets her son's attention before going forward. Listening is most important because critical matters are at hand.

Hearing is a physical function; the listening process is a mental function, used by the human brain, to evaluate what is being said, and filter out the unimportant information.

The human brain has filters in it to separate the important things said or information given is clear, so it is understood by the receiver. Humans hear so many things, but do not always listen, but filters out the non-essential aspects of any information and keep the beneficial features of that information. King Lemuel's mother purposed three questions:

> **What my son?**
> **What the son of my womb?**
> **What the son of my vows?**

She is asking and answering the questions. What actions or steps should you take in life when choosing a mate or in a relationship with a woman whether it is his wife, his friend, close acquaintance, or women around him. In the words of Solomon, "*My son, hear the instruction of thy father, and forsake not the law of thy mother,*" [*Proverbs 1:8*].

And "*Hear, ye children, the instruction of a father, and attend to know understanding. For I give you good doctrine, forsake ye not my law. For I was my father's son, tender and only beloved in the sight of my mother. He taught me also, and said unto me, let thine heart retain my words: keep my commandments, and live. Get wisdom, get understanding: forget it not; neither decline from the words of my mouth. My son, hear the instruction of thy father, and forsake not the law of thy mother,*" [*Proverbs 4:1–5*].

A King must be cognizant of the people in his inner circle; it is easy for his reputation to be damaged. The King sets the moral example or conduct necessary. The dangers of not knowing those who are closet to us, what their intents are; we can unknowingly allow their attitudes or mannerism to become part of our character, which can be detrimental. The Scripture reminds us to, "*Be not deceived: evil communications corrupt good manners,*" [I Corinthians 15:33].

The company we keep often judges us; the company we keep will judge us. The company he keeps also judges a King/leader, as well that expectation of him being careful of who he allows close to him, because he is King/leader, raises the bar to a higher standard.

Saul, the King, in *[I Samuel 15:14-23]*, erred in his judgment by fearing the people rather than fearing the consequences of his actions before God. Saul, because of the fear of the people disobeyed God and did not destroy all the Amorites as God instructed including all the livestock. Listen to his response when called into question by Samuel for his disobedience of God's command, *"And Saul said unto Samuel, "I have sinned: for I have transgressed the Commandments of the Lord, and thy words: because I feared the people; and obeyed their voice,"* [I Samuel 15:14-23].

"When words are many, transgressions are not lacking, but whosoever restrain his lips is prudent. The tongue of the righteous is choice silver; the heart of the wicked is of little worth. The lips of righteous feed many, but fools die for the lack of sense, "[Proverbs 10:19-21].

"The words of a man's mouth are deep waters; the fountain of wisdom is a bubbling brook. It is not good to be partial to the wicked or to deprive the righteous of justice. A fool's lips walk into a fight, and the mouth invites a beating. A fool's mouth is his ruin, and his lips are a snare to his soul," [Proverbs 18:4-7].

Temptation can overtake a King, even to the defiance of God. Judging righteously is necessary in all areas of a Kings' reign. We know from Scripture that God did not excuse Saul's error in judgment, but he suffered the consequences of his action by the loss of God's favor.

[The temptation to heed the voice of others is also a tool of Satan].

It is not above the possibility that a King can be led off track. A King is yet human and subject to all the weaknesses inherent to man because of sin. We have the example of King Solomon with the many interactions with women allowing idol worship to taint his true worship of God, "*But King Solomon loved many foreign women, as well as the daughter of Pharaoh: women of the Moabites, Ammonites, Edomites, Sidonians, and Hittites—from the nations of whom the Lord had said to the children of Israel, "You shall not intermarry with them, nor they with you. Surely, they will turn away your hearts after their gods." Solomon clung to these in love. And he had seven hundred wives, princesses, and three hundred concubines; and his wives turned away his heart. For it was so, when Solomon was old, that his wives turned his heart after other gods; and his heart was not loyal to the Lord his God, as was the heart of his father David. For Solomon went after Ashtoreth the goddess of the Sidonians, and after Milcom the abomination of the Ammonites."*

"*Solomon did evil in the sight of the Lord, and did not fully follow the Lord, as did his father David. Then Solomon built a high place for Chemosh the abomination of Moab, on the hill that is east of Jerusalem, and for Molech the abomination of the people of Ammon. And he did likewise for all his foreign wives, who burned incense and sacrificed to their gods.*

"*So, the Lord became angry with Solomon, because his heart had turned from the Lord God of Israel, who had appeared to him twice, and had commanded him concerning this thing, that he should not go after other gods; but he did not keep what the Lord had commanded. Therefore, the Lord said to Solomon, "Because you have done this, and have not kept My covenant and My statutes, which I have commanded you, I will surely tear the kingdom away from you and give it to your servant. Nevertheless, I will not do it in your days, for the sake of your father David; I will tear it out of the hand of your son. However, I will not tear away the whole kingdom; I will give one tribe to your son for the sake of My servant David, and for the sake of Jerusalem which I have chosen," [I Kings 11:1-13].*

Solomon in his wisdom also reminds us to, "*Remember now thy creator in the days of thy youth while the evil days come not, nor the years draw nigh, when thy shall say, I have no pleasure in them,*" [Ecclesiastics 12:1].

Solomon wisely penned this sage advice. Using your youth to party and have a fun time, enjoy whatever or with whomever you like, spending your youth in fun and folly is a waste of the purpose for which God put man here for; waiting until we get old, and things of this world no longer interest us and using our energy for everything pleasurable rather than using it to serve God, is Vanity.

"The whole duty of man is to fear God and keep His Commandments," *[Ecclesiastics 12:3].*

The end results are vanity and judgment. Solomon wrote this from experience. He tasted and tested folly and life to its fullest.

King Lemuel's mother did not desire the son of her womb, which is as close of a bond a mother can have with a child, to follow down the same path of fun and folly. A mother carries that child nine months. She protects, she feed that child; she is instructing that child while in her womb with her temperament, her emotional state, every decision she makes she has that child in her womb in mind; she talks with her child, she rubs and pats her stomach, all of this is training her child. The point here, she is protecting her child before he comes into the world, and she want to protect that child after birth and throughout his/her life.

A woman never stops being a mother.

The duty of a mother is to keep her child safe. Mother's giving safe advice, she vows before that bundle of joy is born to protect her child and teach him to worship God and be a faithful servant in His Kingdom.

We read of an example of a mother dedicating her child to the service of the Lord, *"And she vowed a vow, and said, O Lord of hosts, if thou wilt indeed look on the affliction of thine handmaid, and remember me, and not forget thine handmaid, but wilt give unto thine handmaid a man child, then I will give him unto the Lord all the days of his life, and there shall no razor come upon his head,"* *[I Samuel 1:11].*

Hannah made a vow promising God if she had a child, she would dedicate him to His service. She kept Samuel until he was weaned and did what she vowed. We know from Scripture Samuel was raised in the temple. A mother's love is evident in both King Lemuel's mother and Samuel's mother. They could have chosen another path but did not. Scripture warns us, *"When thou vowest a vow unto God, defer not to pay it; for He hath no pleasure in fools: pay that which thou hast vowed. Better is it that thou shouldest not vow, than that thou shouldest vow and not pay,"* *[Ecclesiastics 5:4-5].*

Moses warns as well, *"When thou shalt vow a vow unto the Lord thy God, thou shalt not slack to pay it: for the Lord, thy God will surely require it of thee; and it would be sin in thee,"* *[Deuteronomy 23:21].*

Vowing and breaking that vow is dangerous and incurs God's wrath.

We have nothing with which to pay when that payment is due if we break our vow. God becomes angry at our voice and that can lead to our destruction spiritually and physically. Hannah knew this; she like King Lemuel's mother loved her child and wanted the best for him. The world can only offer us trouble because it is the playground of our chief adversary.

King Lemuel's mother did not want him to have what we know today as a shock and awe moment or moments overtime. A mother wants her son to be commonsensical thinking through situations that come before him in life/his throne, without making a hasty judgement, she wants him to judge righteously and rationally.

Wisdom comes overtime. There are two types of wisdom it will either be worldly (sensual) or spiritual (godly).

It is wise to be aware of how the world is around us and the evil that Satan perpetrates. Worldly wisdom is not what we live by; this is what Lemuel's mother wanted him to understand. It brings no peaceful end nor is it pleasing to God. Worldly wisdom is sensual, demonic and has only a feature; there is no benefit to this type of wisdom, "*This wisdom descendeth not from above, but is earthly, sensual, devilish. For where envying and strife is, there is confusion and every evil work,*" *[James 3:15-16].*

Spiritual wisdom is beneficial both in this world and in eternity. We live according to the commands of God and not of this world, "*But the wisdom that is from above is first pure, then peaceable, gentle, and easy to be intreated, full of mercy and good fruit, without partiality, and without hypocrisy,*" *[James 3:17].*

A wise mother will instruct her son guiding his life while he is young until he has matured to a point in his life when application … full application is needed.

Solomon warns that leaders or mainstream people are to be judged righteously, which a king or ruler should make no distinction between right and wrong regardless who it is poor or wealthy, friend, or foe; a leader cannot allow himself to became an oppressor or a tyrant ruling over a kingdom or his people, nor use his power to oppress the poor that cannot help themselves, "*As a roaring lion, and a raging bear; so is a wicked ruler over the poor people. The prince that wanteth understanding is also a great oppressor; but he that hateth covetousness shall prolong his days,*" *[Proverbs 28:15-16].*

Solomon warns further that for any amount regardless how small, man will do what it takes to have it. Anything that will increase his riches or power he will do, *"To have respect of person is not good; and for a piece of bread that man will transgress,"* *[Proverbs 28:11].*

Yet on the other hand, *"The King that faithfully judgeth the poor, his throne shall be ever established,"* *[Proverbs 29:14].*

Moses warns that, *"Ye shall do no unrighteousness in judgment: thou shalt not respect the person of the poor, nor honor the person of the mighty: but in righteousness shall thou judge thy neighbor,"* *[Leviticus 19:15].*

Listen to Moses warning to the judges, *"And I charged you judges at that time, saying, "Hear the causes between your brethren, and judge righteously between every man and his brother, and the stranger that is with him,"* *[Deuteronomy 1:16].*

Moses also taught, *"Thou shalt not wrest judgment; thou shalt not respect person, neither take a gift: for a gift doth blind the eyes of the wise, and prevent the words of the righteous,"* *[Deuteronomy 16:19].*

This warning is like unto the warning of Solomon, *"For a piece of bread a man will trespass,"* *[Ibid].*

John, the Apostle, gave the same warning, *"Judge not according to the appearance, but judge righteous judgment,"* *[John 7:24].*

Also, a king or person who has no vision leads the people in a dangerous direction for his inability to discern right or wrong or defying the laws of God, *"Where there is no vision, the people perish: but he that keepth the law, happy is he,"* *[Proverbs 29:18].*

King Lemuel's mother taught him in reference to extramarital affairs, lessons in reframe (chastity) and self-control (temperance).

V3: "Give not thy strength unto women, nor to the ways to that which destroys Kings."

A woman diverted Solomon's father, King David's focus. It began with an improper act by him watching a female without her knowledge on [her] roof taking a bath ... peaking his desire for her to the point of committing murder to cover their sin of adultery causing a domino effect by breaking one of the Ten Commandments of God's Law, *"Thy shall not commit adultery,"* [Exodus 20:14].

Bathsheba was another man's wife, Uriah, the Hittite; his one little Ewe. David desiring her beyond his ability of self-control committed adultery first in his heart and then physically finally bringing the sin in full circumference, which harmed his reputation and incurred God's wrath. This commandment applies to all regardless of the period-of-time we live in and is without respect of person.

"And it came to pass in an evening tide, that David arose from off his bed, and walked upon the roof of the king's house: and from the roof he saw a woman washing herself; and the woman was very beautiful to look upon. And David sent and enquired after the woman. And one said, Is not this Bathsheba, the daughter of Eliam, the wife of Uriah the Hittite? And David sent messengers and took her; and she came in unto him, and he lay with her; for she was purified from her uncleanness: and she returned unto her house. And the woman conceived, and sent and told David, and said, I am with child," [2 Samuel 11:2-4].

The punishment was painful and unbearable that David suffered, the first child of David and Bathsheba did not live. Let us not forget that two people commit adultery, not one.

Bathsheba was as guilty as King David.

Though she may have taken a bath before she returned to her home, did not wash away the sin she indulged in with the King, *"For she was purified from her uncleanness,"* [Ibid].

We read the Biblical account of David and Bathsheba's sin, which included the death of Uriah the Hittite, because he (David) lusted after his wife. His sin exposed by Nathan, the Prophet, in the way of comparison to a man with one little Ewe. Though David repented, his sin was costly.

David's sin had a long reaching effect on his family, his son Amnon loved his sister Tamar and forced her to lie with him, afterwards he hated her, *[2 Samuel 13:1-14]*. Absalom killed his half-brother Amnon, because he raped his sister Tamar, and (he) Absalom, was hanged by his hair on a Terebinth Tree while fleeing, *[2 Samuel 18:6-19]*.

Jesus said when asked this question about adultery, *"But I say unto you, that whosoever looketh on a woman to lust after her hath committed adultery with her already in his heart,"* *[Matthew 28:28]*.

Then again in contrast, Job considered his Master in Heaven and the danger of not doing right as a leader. He knew that lust comes in many forms not just the lust of the flesh, but also for the material possessions in this life usually one accompanies the other. Lust that feeds the soul destroy all of you and defiles the conscience which angers God, *"If mine heart have been deceived by a woman, or if I have laid wait at my neighbor's door; then let my wife grind unto another, and let others bow down upon her. For this is a heinous crime; yea, it is an iniquity to be punished by the judges. For it is a fire that consumeth to destruction and would root out all mine increase. If I did despise the cause of my manservant or of my maidservant, when they contended with me; What then shall I do when God riseth up? and when He visiteth, what shall I answer Him? Did not He that made me in the womb make him? and did not one fashion us in the womb?"* *[Job 1:9-15]*.

The destruction of leaders, Presidents, and ordinary men are still present in this day and time as in Old Testament time are still being side-tracked by multiple women in their lives. We are reminded what John, the Apostle wrote through the inspiration of the Holy Spirit, *"All that is in the world is the lust of the flesh, the lust of the eye, and the pride of life,"* *[Ibid]*.

David, Solomon, Samson, and others were conquered by all three.

Satan includes them (lust of the flesh, lust of the eye, and the pride of life), in his buffet of pleasures making them look so attractive, but they are more destructive in the end as Solomon warns, *"Vanities of Vanities, all is Vanity,"* *[Ibid]*.

Satan's morsels of pleasures become spiritual liabilities eventually in this life and even more so a permanency in eternity. He lies morbidly and falsely. People of God cannot allow themselves to fall prey to his lies and deceit. Jesus said, *"Ye are of your father the devil, and the lusts of your father ye will do. He was a murderer from the beginning, and abode not in the truth, because there is no truth in him. When he speaketh a lie, he speaketh of his own: for he is a liar, and the father of it,"* *[John 8:44]*.

Man's desire and lust for the pleasures of this world that Satan makes fluidly available sandwiches them in and will here, and for an eternity, lead to spiritual destruction, if not corrected.

King Lemuel's mother wanted the King to stay focused. I am sure she reminded her son that King David allowed himself to be pulled into an affair which we know from Scripture clouded his judgment. A King's ability to reason must remain on focus. If his thoughts are on multiple women or an adulterous woman, or his desires for physical pleasure; his judgment is not sound. *[2 Samuel 11-12].*

In the guidelines Moses wrote for a Kings of Israel to adhere to was at the forefront of his mother's mind, *"Neither shall he multiply wives to himself that his heart turn not away. Neither shall he multiply to himself silver and gold,"* [Deuteronomy 17:17].

- ➤ **Does not women, gold, and silver all go hand in hand, when one multiply so does the other?**
- ➤ **Are not all three of these just as destructive?**

On the other hand, an adulterous woman is usually who causes a King to stumble – or more than one wife. Solomon had many wives and concubines. His father David had eight wives. So many women pulling in the opposite directions will prevent the king from focusing on his God-given duties.

The spirit of envy and jealousy will exist when a King has more than one woman or more than one wife in the picture, *"Death and Destruction are never satisfied, and neither are human eyes." [Proverbs 27:20].* Application of *[I John 2:15-17]* can be made here, *"Lust of the eye, lust of the flesh, and the pride of life."*

Also, Scripture reminds us that, *"A sound heart is the life of the flesh; but envy the rottenness of the bone," [Proverbs 14:30]*

- ➤ **How can a King focus on the matters at hand when there are so many wives who has a pull on his attention or bid for his affection?**
- ➤ **At some point, it will become an all-out competition between the wives and the women involved!**

Each one competing for attention from the King. David like Solomon's attention was pulled away from God. Trying to please more than one wife is a sneaky trap set by Satan, especially if you are a servant of God. Envy and jealousy or the overflow effect of it, will rob us of who we are, Satan uses it to [his] advantage.

41

King Lemuel's mother wanted him to cement his actions and be wise. She wanted him to take heed, be mindful of his duties and responsibilities.

Solomon poses this question, *"And why wilt thou, my son, be ravished with a strange woman and embrace the bosom of a stranger,"* [Proverbs 5:20].

Strange women bring with them many sorrows and woes, *"My son give me thine heart, and let thine eyes observe my ways. So, also lieth in wait as a prey, and increaseth the transgressions among men. Who hath woe? Who hath sorrow? Who hath contentions? Who has babbling? Who hath wounds without cause? Who hath redness of eye? For a whore is a deep pit and a strange woman is a narrow pit,"* [Proverbs 23:26-28].

Listen to the warning Jesus gave John the Apostle to tell the leaders in the Church at Thyatira, *"Notwithstanding, I have a few things against thee because thou suffereth that woman Jezebel, which calleth herself a prophetess, to teach and to seduce my servants to commit fornication, and to eat things offered to idols. And I gave her space to repent of her fornication; and she repented not. Behold, I will cast her into a bed, and they that commit adultery with her into great tribulation; except they repent of their deeds,"* [Revelations 2:20-22].

We as servants of God cannot despise the mystery of God nor can we embrace the mystery of Satan and the evil each of his actions brings with it. We cannot choose which of God's commands we want to obey. There is no truth in anything Satan does; he is a liar and was from the beginning. We cannot follow nor even investigate the doctrine of Satan, anything not of God is of Satan.

However, we can know and need to investigate (study) what God requires of us, as His children.

Satan's doctrine is moveable, ever-moving, changeable, the depths are unfathomable it is not in man to know the depts and pits of his evil, it is an unbearable burden that we cannot carry; if he gets you in his grips never desiring to let you go will continually add (stacking) to that burden of sin.

Jezebel is a pseudonym for a display of certain types of characteristics. We read of the evil acts of both women in Scripture name Jezebel. We can look at Jezebel from the viewpoint, of one who have an evil corrupt spirit that desires to live a life that is not pleasing to God. Involving or allowing ourselves to be pulled in gives no path back. King Lemuel's mother wanted him to know, to be aware of the dangers of a strange woman and an adulterous woman.

Samson is another example of man a woman led from true obedience to God. He rendered his strength to a woman. The influence of a strange woman can deplete a King (leader) of their strength. Samson became conceited and begin to pursue Philistine women. He had physical supernatural strength, but one weakness emotionally, he loved women.

Stepping outside of God's plan cost him his strength, and his eyes, *"And the children of Israel did evil again in the sight of the Lord; and the Lord delivered them into the hand of the Philistines forty years. And there was a certain man of Zorah, of the family of the Danites, whose name was Manoah; and his wife was barren, and bare not. And the angel of the Lord appeared unto the woman, and said unto her, behold now, thou art barren, and bearest not: but thou shalt conceive, and bear a son. Now therefore beware, I pray thee, and drink not wine nor strong drink, and eat not any unclean thing: For, lo, thou shalt conceive, and bear a son; and no razor shall come on his head: for the child shall be a Nazarite unto God from the womb," [Ibid].*

Abstinence was essential and he let his guard down, strong drink, pleasure, and the disease of a loose tongue revealed the source of his strength at the pleas of Delilah, *"Please tell me the source of your strength how you can be tied up and subdued," [Judges 16:6].*

Discussing the source of his strength was in direct disobedience to the command of God. Samson's mother taught him what he needed to do to protect his strength and its source; he forgot his mother's teaching and fell prey to a devious woman.

Delilah sold the information to the Philistines of his amazing strength for more than five thousand pieces of silver, *"And the lords of the Philistines came up unto her, and said unto her, entice him, and see wherein his great strength lieth, and by what means we may prevail against him, that we may bind him to afflict him; and we will give thee every one of us eleven hundred pieces of silver," [Judges 16:5].*

Betrayal comes in all shapes, forms, and types. Judas covenanted with the Chief Priest of the Sanhedrin for information and location of Christ Our Savior for thirty pieces of silver, *"Then one of the twelve, called Judas Iscariot, went unto the chief priests, and said unto them, what will ye give me, and I will deliver Him unto you? And they covenanted with him for thirty pieces of silver," [Matthew 26:14-15].*

➢ **Samson's heart was betrayed by his wife, a Philistine woman, when she discovered the answer to the riddle and told the Philistines; why would he not know (or at least be suspicious of) another woman of the Philistine people (Delilah) would do the same?**

The Philistines were their enemies of who he was delivering his people. He ignored his father and mother with the first Philistine woman, and it cost him; again, by choosing not to be obedient to his parents, *"Forget not the teaching of your mother,"* [Ibid].

Who will a man or woman betray or what will a man give in exchange for his soul is a question in all centuries? Jesus counseled the people in one of His Sermons, *"What does it profit a man to gain the whole world, yet forfeit his soul? Or what will a man give in exchange for his soul?"* [Mark 8:36-37].

➢ **Christ asked these questions! How would you answer?**

The beauty of Samson is evident with the hair that his strength emanates from – no razor or scissors had touched his head. Samson's mother kept her vow to God.

Samson was blinded by the desire to possess Delilah … Delilah was blinded by her greed and lust for money. One cannot feed on lust, greed, and power, that diet is a recipe for destruction and failure of a king/leader and their kingdom.

Fraternizing with sin and those who love to partake therein, a king or leader must be aware of the baggage of danger it and they bring with them.

Samson was blinded in two ways: by his lust for a woman as well as being blinded physically. The Philistines put his eyes out. Fear of power and desire to have power has always been since the beginning of time. The Philistines believed if they could find the source of his power, they could destroy him, and Israel's delivers would not pose a problem for them. They knew he was judge and servant of the Most High God.

Samson forgot the teachings of his mother failing to take heed to the lessons she taught him and walk circumspectly as we are warned to do in Scripture.

The days now are just as they were then. We cannot forget one minute we have an adversary, *"See then that ye walk circumspectly, not as fools, but as wise, redeeming the time, because the days are evil. Wherefore be ye not unwise but understanding what the will of the Lord is. And be not drunk with wine, wherein is excess; but be filled with the Spirit; speaking to yourselves in psalms and hymns and spiritual songs, singing and making melody in your heart to the Lord; giving thanks always for all things unto God and the Father in the name of our Lord Jesus Christ; submitting yourselves one to another in the fear of God," [Ephesians 5:15-21].*

Satan is alive and well and his goal and focus is destroying as many lives of God's people as he can through deception as he did Samson with a strange woman.

Solomon in Proverbs asked the following questions, *"Can a man take fire in his bosom, and his clothes not be burned? Can one go upon hot coals, and his feet not be burned?" [Proverbs 6:27-28].*

Those in leadership can resist temptation or must resist temptation and not lose themselves to the things of the world or the needs of their bodies or let the desires of their hearts lead them astray.

Joseph resisted the temptation that Potiphar's wife heaped upon him, *"And she caught him by his garment, saying, "Lie with me: and he left his garment in her hand, and fled, and got him out," [Genesis 39:12].*

It takes prudence and wisdom to recognize that a strange woman has no good intentions, but they are evil; her intent is subverting a King's mind in a manner that is not pleasing to God. He is wise to avoid her with all expediency not allowing her even an audience, *"A prudent man forseeth the evil, and hideth himself, but the simple pass on, and are punished,"* [Proverbs 22:3].

It is a plus for a King when he serves God through knowledge and wisdom. This warning is, *"To deliver thee from the strange woman, even from the strange woman that flattereth with her words," [Proverbs 2:16].*

Solomon warned that, *"For her house inclineth unto death, and the path unto the dead. None that go unto her return again, neither take they hold of the path of life," [Proverbs 2:18-19].*

Women are dangerous who has intents that are evil … evil company leads to fleshly lust, defiling the body, which wars against the soul. Our bodies are the temple where the Holy Spirit dwells; He cannot dwell in an unclean temple.

King Lemuel's mother wanted him to remember the following: this wisdom applies to this generation as well:

> **It is almost impossible to recover from the snares of sin!**
> **Sin is not willing to loosen its grip once it has you!**
> **Satan is a perfect orchestrator of destruction!**
> **Satan has nothing to lose. He is already lost for an eternity!**

We are to keep in mind that, God did not rip the Kingdom from Solomon when he went after strange women and worshipped other gods, because of His promise to David, *"Wherefore, the Lord said unto Solomon, "forasmuch as this is done of thee, and thou hast not kept my covenant and my status, which I have commanded thee, I will surely rend the kingdom from thee, and will give it to thy servant,"* [I Kings 11:11].

"Nevertheless, for the sake of your father David, I will not do it during your lifetime; I will tear it of the hand of your son," [I Kings 11:12].

Paul warns the people of God to separate themselves from the world. There has to be a distinct difference in the actions of the people of God and the actions of the world or the world cannot distinguish God's people from anyone else who lives in pleasure while they are alive, *"Wherefore come out from among them, and be ye separate said the Lord, and touch not the unclean thing, and I will receive you,"* [2 Corinthians 6:17].

Solomon, learned from his experience that all that is in the world is vanity and we should leave it behind us and serve God in truth, knowledge, and understanding; admonishes us to, *"Leave your folly behind; and you will live; walk in the ways of understanding,"* [Proverbs 7:6].

Solomon further warns about strange women in this manner:

"For the lips of a strange woman drips as a honeycomb and her mouth is smother than oil," [Proverbs 5:3].

"But her end is bitter as wormwood, sharp as a two-edged sword," [Proverbs 5:4].

"Her feet go down to death; her steps take hold on hell," [Proverbs 5:5].

"Lest thou shouldest ponder the path of life, her ways are moveable, that thou canst not know them," [Proverbs 5:6].

"Hear me now therefore, O ye children, and depart not from the words of my mouth," [Proverbs 5:7].

"Remove thy way far from her and come not nigh the door of her house: lest thou give thine honor unto other, and thy years unto the cruel," [Proverbs 5:8].

The mouth of an adulterous woman dripping like a honeycomb gives us a full understanding of what Solomon's warning is like. We know that honey is one of the sweetest food items on earth, yet it is tasty and desired by so many can have a negative effect on you: honey when consumed in substantial amounts can make you sick physically. When drawn away by the sweet words of an adulterous woman in the end is just as bitterly destructive as consuming too much honey.

V4: "It is not for Kings, O Lemuel, it is not for Kings to drink wine; nor for princes strong drink."

King Lemuel's mother, as with the first verse, because of the importance of the wisdom being imparted thought it necessary to repeat the fact that wine (strong drink) is not something (habit or pleasure) a King should indulge in. The destruction has come to many through their indulgence in the loathsomeness of this vice.

This evil can be compared to a vile woman both are destructive and can ruin a King and destroy his kingdom. King Lemuel's mother compare contrast these two evils that can quickly destroy a promising ruler, "*In the twilight, in the evening, in the black and dark night: And, behold, there met him a woman with the attire of an harlot, and subtil of heart.(She is loud and stubborn; her feet abide not in her house: Now is she without, now in the streets, and lieth in wait at every corner).*

"*So she caught him, and kissed him, and with an impudent face said unto him, I have peace offerings with me; this day have I payed my vows.*"

"*Therefore came I forth to meet thee, diligently to seek thy face, and I have found thee. I have decked my bed with coverings of tapestry, with carved works, with fine linen of Egypt. I have perfumed my bed with myrrh, aloes, and cinnamon. Come, let us take our fill of love until the morning: let us solace ourselves with loves. For the goodman is not at home, he is gone on a long journey: He hath taken a bag of money with him, and will come home at the day appointed. With her much fair speech she caused him to yield, with the flattering of her lips she forced him,*" [Proverbs 7:9-21].

In order that a King, Prince, Judge, any leader of a people be successful in performing his/their duties and care for his/their Kingdom or the ones that look to him/them for direction, must keep in mind as the Preacher reminds us that, "*Wine is a mocker and strong drink is a rage and whosoever is deceived thereby is not wise,*" [Proverbs 20:1].

Kings desire the enjoyment and excitement that comes with strong drink just as others. In this respect, there is no difference in the common man and the King. The wine/strong drink has the same effect. The Scripture tells us, "*Whosoever is deceived,*" [Ibid].

The comparing and contrasting of wine's deceit and the deceit of a vile woman is clearly pointed out by King Lemuel's mother. The destructive effect is the same.

V5: Lest thou drink and forget what is decreed depriving all the oppressed of justice."

"Do not drink wine nor strong drink, thou, nor thy sons with thee, when ye go into the tabernacle of the congregation, lest ye die; it shall be a statue forever throughout your generation," [Leviticus 10:9].

There is a woe to those who are mighty and in power. Listen to the Prophet Isaiah, *"Woe unto them that are mighty to drink wine, and men of strength to mingle strong drink," [Isaiah 5:22].*

It is not befitting for a king to drink or mingle strong drink. Liquor or wine can reduce a person's reasoning and judging abilities to a destructive level. When a king's reasoning abilities are reduced, his understanding is not sound, or logic is captivated by the persuasive voice and arms of wine and strong drink, will bring him to sure destruction. Her strong arms will hold him until his judgment is completely gone.

A point about the abuse of power that a King/leader has; in addition to the abuse caused by strong drink: [A use of a King's power, along with strong drink, other irrational thoughts as well can cause a King/leader to be outside of himself and become jealous, vindictive, and cruel as well as we have seen in many of the Biblical examples depending upon the situation.]

This quote from Henry is a sobering thought, "Unbridled wrath armed with unlawful power often carries men to absurd (illogical) cruelties," [*Matthew Henry Commentary 1710*].

Herod's used his power and authority in the destruction of all male babies in Bethlehem and surrounding cities trying to rid the world of who thought would be his competition, did not understand the Spiritual Kingdom Christ came to establish was not earthly, *"Then Herod, when he saw that he was mocked of the wise men, was exceeding wroth, and sent forth, and slew all the children that were in Bethlehem, and in all the coasts thereof, from two years old and under, according to the time which he had diligently inquired of the wise men," [Matthew 2:16-18].*

Isaiah, the Prophet also wrote that the Priests and Prophets who indulged were not themselves, *"But they also have erred through wine, and through strong drink are out of the way; the Priest and the Prophets have erred through strong drink, they swallowed up wine, they are out of the way through strong drink, they erred in vision, they stumble in judgment,"* [Isaiah 28:7].

> ➢ **Could they amend the error in judgment made?**
> ➢ **Were their minds clear so that they might see the vision and understand what God would have them to do?**
> ➢ **Stumbling in judgment is costly, usually to the person (people) to whom you have charge over, could they reverse the cost of the drunken error?**
> ➢ **Could Herod reverse the cost of pain and suffering to the overall community, because of his fear and thirst to retain power?**
> ➢ **A King's power used in a negative manner is costly, could the mothers and fathers in Bethlehem ever recover from the cruelty?**

Luke, the Physician, gave an example of what a servant of God looks like when strong drink is absent from his life when speaking of John, the Baptist, *"For he shall be great in the sight of the Lord, and shall drink neither wine nor strong drink; and he shall be filled with the Holy Ghost, even from his mother's womb,"* [Luke 1:15].

John the Baptist thoughts, reasonings, and judgments were made from a clear mind; he did not pervert judgment nor did he stumble or err in when he preached repentance to the people. He was at himself throughout his short life on earth never *'out of the way'* as the priests and prophets were spoken of by Moses and Isaiah; but served God with a clear and focused mind.

Jesus said concerning trying to live in both worlds, *"No man can serve two masters: for either he will hate the one and love the other; or else he will hold to the one and despise the other. Ye cannot serve God and mammon,"* [Matthew 6:24].

> ➢ **How can one serve God and do His bidding without a clear mind?**
> ➢ **There is a way that God has for Kings, Prophets, or his people to walk, how can a king/leader walk that way if they are partaking of the vices of Satan?**

John the Baptist, like Samson, is another example of a servant of God who was born for a specific purpose in God's service. Gabriel announced to Zechariah that his prayers had been heard and that he would have a son, *"He will be a joy and delight to you, and many will rejoice because of his birth, for he will be great in the sight of the Lord. He is never to take wine or other fermented drink, and he will be filled with the Holy Spirit even before he is born. He will bring back many of the people of Israel to the Lord their God. And he will go on before the Lord, in the spirit and power of Elijah, to turn the hearts of the parents to their children and the disobedient to the wisdom of the righteous—to make ready a people prepared for the Lord," [Luke 1:14-17].*

Paul, the Apostle, also warns that, *"It is good neither to eat flesh, nor to drink wine, nor anything whereby they brother stumbleth, or is offended, or is made weak,"* [Romans 14:21].

V6: *"Give strong drink unto him that is ready to perish, and wine unto those that be of heavy heart."*

This verse indicated not just a flirtation with failure but a full embracement of a destructive relationship. Strong drink here is expressed as not being for a King it is a slow road to ruin. Wine and strange women are a recipe for disaster for a King.

(At this juncture, just to make an obvious point, wine (strong drink) strange women are destructive paths for any man), *"And wine that maketh glad the heart of man, and oil to make his face to shine, and bread which strengthen man's heart,"* [Psalms 104:15].

God can supply all our needs. Man's desire to over-indulge and put too much focus on pleasure on the misuse of food and strong drink are not pleasing to God. We do not need strong drink to help us with the challenging time. We can look to God for our encouragement and strength so that we might stay within the confines of righteousness so as to do His will.

A King is responsible for the welfare of his people. The people of his kingdom look to him for care and sustenance. He must keep a clear head and remain purposeful.

King Lemuel's mother wanted her son, who she raised in the admonition and nurture of the Lord, to be aware that wine could destroy his Throne. Wine like a strange woman takes his attention away from his duties. A King's responsibilities are difficult in and of themselves; he needs no additional complications added to them by overindulging in the evils of this world. A King had to be careful even more so than the ordinary man, *"It is good neither to eat flesh, nor to drink wine, nor any thing whereby thy brother stumbleth, or is offended, or is made weak,"* [Ibid].

"Woe unto them that rise up early in the morning, that they may follow strong drink; that continue until night, till wine inflame them!" [Isaiah 5:11].

"But they also have erred through wine, and through strong drink are out of the way; the priests and the prophets have erred through strong drink, they are swallowed up of wine, they are out of the way through strong drink; they err in vision, they stumble in judgment," [Ibid].

We see the same instructions given to leaders in today, *"Likewise the deacons must be grave, not double-tongued, not given to much wine, not greedy of filthy lucre,"* [I Timothy 3:8].

Wine and money causes humans to commit all manners of evil against their neighbor.

King Belshazzar, son of King Nebuchadnezzar, drank to his destruction. Partaking of strong drink before his subjects and with the subjects of his kingdom, in vessels his father King Nebuchadnezzar had taken from the temple which was in Jerusalem; that the King and his princes, his wives, and his concubines drank therein. They drank wine and praised the gods of gold, and silver, of brass, of iron, of wood, and of stone, defiling the sacred items from the temple angering The Most High God, *"Then they brought the golden vessels that were taken out of the temple of the House of God which was at Jerusalem. And the king and his officials, his wives and his concubines drank from them. They drank wine and praised the gods of gold and of silver, of bronze, of iron, of wood, and of stone,"* [Daniel 5:3].

He and his wives, princes, concubines, drank to their destruction, *"In the same hour came forth fingers of a man's hand, and wrote over against the candlestick upon the plaster of the wall of the King's Palace; and the King saw the part of the hand that wrote,"* [Daniel 5:5].

Daniel interpreted the handwriting on the wall, and this was the interpretation because he (Belshazzar) had not humbled himself before God as his father King Nebuchadnezzar finally did when God humbled him.

Hear the reason Daniel told Belshazzar for the mysterious hand, *"And thou his son Belshazzar, has not humbled thine head though thou knoweth this, but has lifted up thyself against the Lord of Heaven; and they have bought the vessels of His House before thee, and thou, and thy lords, they wives, and thy concubines, have drunk wine in them; and thou hast praised the gods of silver, and gold, of brass, and iron, wood, and stone, which see not nor hear, nor know: and the God in whose hand thy breathe is and whose all thy ways has thou not glorified,"* [Daniel 5:22-23].

Pride, arrogance, partying, lust, and licentiousness by products of this indulgence are all bad examples that can be seen if wine and strong drink is involved, which is not appropriate for a king, whose influence is gone because he can be and allowed himself to be influenced by that society of people around him who indulges in this type of living.

Daniel explained the meaning of the writing, *"Then was the part of the hand sent from Him; and this writing was written. And this is the writing that was written,* Mene, Mene, Tekel, Upharsin. *This is the interpretation of the thing:* Mene; *God hath numbered thy kingdom and finished it.* Tekel; *Thou art weighed in the balances, and art found wanting.* PERES: *Thy kingdom is divided, and given to the Medes and Persians,"* [Daniel 5:24–28].

God ripped the kingdom away from Belshazzar; he was killed that night.

Job reminds us, *"Even as I have seen, they that plow iniquity and sow wickedness, reaps the same,"* [Job 4:8].

> ➤ Are not the lessons of those long gone enough for the hearer and those who comes after them examples of the danger of defying the Commandments and worshipping other gods rather than the one and only true God of Heaven, maker of all things, and ruler over the universe?

V7: *"Let him drink and forget his poverty and remember his misery no more."*

This is a continuation of the warning we read in **[V6]**, *"Who hath woe? who hath sorrow? who hath contentions? who hath babbling? who hath wounds without cause? who hath redness of eyes? They that tarry long at the wine; they that go to seek mixed wine. Look not thou upon the wine when it is red, when it giveth his colour in the cup, when it moveth itself aright. At the last it biteth like a serpent, and stingeth like an adder. Thine eyes shall behold strange women, and thine heart shall utter perverse things. Yea, thou shalt be as he that lieth down in the midst of the sea, or as he that lieth upon the top of a mast. They have stricken me, shalt thou say, and I was not sick; they have beaten me, and I felt it not: when shall I awake? I will seek it yet again,"* [Proverbs 23:29-35].

In the Book of Proverb, the Preacher, also, at times employed a bit of irony – it is disdain in a mocking way to convey contempt. It is ironic for a King to drink and forget his poverty. Kings in a kingdom are wealthy. Unless it was a poverty of the spirit or other human-related ailments. Kings rarely suffered from poverty – poverty would be a poor reason for a King to be ruled by drunkenness. How ridiculous it would look for the ruler of a Kingdom to drink and use poverty as a reason for his irresponsibility to his duties and his people.

The Prophet Hosea reminds us, *"Whoredom, wine, and new wine, which takes away the understanding,"* [Hosea 4:11].

Paul reminds us not to allow ourselves to be enslaved by the pleasure of this world. Also, that things and pleasures of this life that we desire, we have a right to take part in, but are not expedient or wise for anyone, but especially a king or leader it is easy to become a slave to that habit; unhealthy habits, wine, and strong drinks are cruel taskmasters. Hear the warnings of the Apostle Paul, *"All things are lawful for me, but not all things are helpful, all things are lawful for me, but I will not be enslaved by anything,"* [I Corinthians 6:12].

V8: *"Open the mouth for the dumb in the curse of all such as are appointed to destruction."*

Speaking for those who cannot for themselves is also the responsibility of a King for the people of his kingdom. He is the protector of all, the leader who can come to the defense of the helpless. We have the poor and helpless in every generation since the beginning of time. The Scripture reminds us of the position that Job took as a leader and the one who others look to for help, *"I was eyes to the blind, and feet was I to the lame: I was a father to the poor; and the cause which I knew not I searched out," [Job 29:15-16].*

Kings who have dignity and rank needs prudence, integrity, and the ability to guide his Kingdom. Good rulers are to be a fear to the evil doers and protector to those who are innocent; he must arm himself with tenacity as well, have the resolve of fairness, and care, for all people without respect of person.

Pride is always a danger in a King. A negative characteristic to be mindful of and to avoid if we want to be pleasing to God. Job was an example of this, though not a King, he was revered, respected, and sought after for his wisdom. He searched for a resolution to all problems.

King Lemuel's mother was wise, he would show wisdom in heeding her advice. A mother will always guide her child in the right direction; she will do no harm, nor do she want harm to come to him. A wise mother looks to God for her wisdom to know how to advise her son wisely in all matters that his steps on the pathway of life might be pleasing to God, and he is not *'out of the way'* of the righteousness of God.

A King who chooses their relationships with people who are being governed by the lust of the flesh, will be displeasing to God. We are constantly reminded that things of the world are not pleasing to God, *"Lust of the flesh, lust of the eye, and the pride of life," [Ibid].*

Solomon expressed those whose words are borne from wisdom in this manner, *"The words of the wise are as goads, and as nails fastened by the master of assemblies, which is given from One Shepherd," [Ecclesiastes 12:11].*

Further he counseled the hearer to, *"Incline your ear and hear the words of the wise – apply your mind to my knowledge," [Proverbs 22:11].*

As well, *"It is better to heed a wise man's rebuke than to listen to the song of fools,"* [Ecclesiastes 7:5].

King Lemuel's mother did not want him to get mired down with ease, as many of the rich and chief men did in that dispensation of time and forget the cause of the poor and innocent. Amos, the Prophet, warns the leaders, kings, princes, and men of means in this way; and it does apply even unto today, *"Woe to them that are at ease in Zion, and trust in the mountain of Samaria, which are named chief of the nations, to whom the house of Israel came! Pass ye unto Calneh (Genesis 10:10), and see; and from thence go ye to Hamath the great (Amos 6:2): then go down to Gath of the Philistines (2 Kings 12:17): be they better than these kingdoms? or their border greater than your border? Ye that put far away the evil day, and cause the seat of violence to come near; that lie upon beds of ivory, and stretch themselves upon their couches, and eat the lambs out of the flock, and the calves out of the midst of the stall; that chant to the sound of the viol, and invent to themselves instruments of musick, like David; that drink wine in bowls, and anoint themselves with the chief ointments: but they are not grieved for the affliction of Joseph. Therefore, now shall they go captive with the first that go captive, and the banquet of them that stretched themselves shall be removed,"* [Amos 6:1-7].

The Prophecy that God gave to Amos to remind the leaders they should be able to see and remember what destruction was bought upon Calneh, Hamath the great, and Gath of the Philistines and see what once beauty and greatness they enjoyed and those who got comfortable in their wealth, trusted in it more than in God, and forgot the poor and innocent, bought upon themselves certain destruction.

King Lemuel's mother did not want him and his kingdom to fall into ruin as others had over the centuries.

Kings or those in authority or has influence uses wisdom when dealing with the evil when it is before them, *"And when Saul sent messengers to take David, she said, "he is sick,"* [I Samuel 19:14].

Michal, David's wife, used wisdom to save David's life from King Saul seeking to slay him because of the evil spirit from the Lord that was upon him, *"And the evil spirit from the Lord was upon Saul, as he sat in his house with his javelin in his hand: and David played with his hand. And Saul sought to smite David even to the wall with the javelin; but he slipped away out of Saul's presence, and he smote the javelin into the wall: and David fled, and escaped that night,"* [I Samuel 19:9-10].

Esther used wisdom to save her people before the King of Persia when they were sought to be annihilated by evil perpetrated by one man, Haman the Agagite, "*Go and gather all the Jews that are present in Shushan, and fast ye for me, and neither eat or drink three days: night or day. I also and my maidens will fast likewise; and so, will I go in unto the King, which is not according to the law: and if I perish, I perish,*" *[Esther 4:16].*

When the request that came to Esther from Mordecai to save her people, she acted in wisdom. Esther's faith moved her to take a risk and advised her people to do likewise that through faith, fasting, and prayer had faith that God would answer their request.

She stood in the gap for the poor and innocent and did not forget from which her blessing came.

The wisdom of a woman shines brightly in the story of Esther the Queen, who herself was a ruler as well. As Esther's people, the Jews, life depended on her, so did the lives of her people on King Xerxes. She risked her life to stand against the empire to make sure her people was safe, because she knew and believed in the one True God and His promises to His people though they were in captivity, were not alone.

V9: "Open they mouth, judge righteously, and plead the cause of the poor and needy.

All who are in authority (a King) or one who judges, are commanded to do judgement without partiality, *"Ye shall do not unrighteousness in judgement; thou shalt not respect the person of the poor, nor honor the person of the mighty; but in righteousness shall thou judge thy neighbor,"* [Leviticus 19:15].

Hear what Moses warned, *"And I charged you judges at that time, say, "Hear the cause between your brethren, and judge righteously between every man and his brother, and the stranger that is with him,"* [Deuteronomy 1:16].

Kings must see that the commands of the law are adhered to. Also execute and see that those laws are conducted fairly and righteously among and between all men and their keeping the royal law, *"If ye fulfil the royal law according to the scripture, thou shalt love thy neighbour as thyself, ye do well,"* [James 2:8].

"Open your mouth for the mute, for the rights of all who are destitute. Open your mouth, judge righteously, defend the rights of the poor and needy," [Proverbs 31:8-9].

Job, faithful servant of God said, *"Because I delivered the poor that cried, and the fatherless, and him that had none to help there was hope,"* [Job 29:12].

Job considered the poor. Our duties as Christians are to show hospitality. He was mindful of God and what was right with charitable behavior toward the poor and needy, *"If I have denied the desires of the poor or let the eyes of the widow grow weary, if I have kept my bread to myself, not sharing it with the fatherless-but from my youth I reared them as a father would, and from my birth I guided the widow-if I have seen anyone perishing for lack of clothing, or the needy without garments, and their hearts did not bless me for warming them with the fleece from my sheep, if I have raised my hand against the fatherless, knowing that I had influence in court, then let my arm fall from the shoulder, let it be broken off at the joint. For I dreaded destruction from God, and for fear of His splendor I could not do such thing,"* [Job 31:16-23].

There was hope among the young, the widows, and all that knew and saw. Righteous leaders give the people hope where there is none, justice when it cannot be had, and safety because life is important to those who are living.

Job showed his faith by his work as we are admonished to do, "*If a brother or sister be naked, and destitute of daily food, and one of you say unto them, depart in peace, be ye warmed and filled; notwithstanding ye give them not those things which are needful to the body; what doth it profit?*" [James 2:15-16].

"*Even so faith if it hath not works, is dead, being alone. Yea, a man may say, thou hast faith, and I have works shew me thy faith without thy works, and I will shew thee my faith by my works,*" [James 2:17-18].

"*But wilt thou know, O vain man, that faith without works is dead? Was not Abraham our father justified by works, when he had offered Isaac his son upon the altar? Seest thou how faith wrought with his works, and by works was faith made perfect? And the scripture was fulfilled which saith, Abraham believed God, and it was imputed unto him for righteousness: and he was called the Friend of God. Ye see then how that by works a man is justified, and not by faith only. Likewise, also was not Rahab the harlot justified by works, when she had received the messengers, and had sent them out another way? For as the body without the spirit is dead, so faith without works is dead also,*" [James 2:20-26].

Even the most hateful of humans requires fairness in judgment. A King must be impartial regardless of his feeling about that person. God gave his only begotten Son for all, including the underserving in our sight.

Only can a King be pleasing to God when he is fair to all regardless of their status in life, "*He judged the cause of the poor and needy; then it was well with him: was not this to know Me? Saith the Lord,*" [Jeremiah 22:16].

If we are to know God and be pleasing, we are to consider and view all men as important and not become respecter of persons in reference to right, wrong, need, the fatherless, the helpless; whether rich of poor; righteous fairness should apply to all; then we can know God, because He is Holy, righteous, judges righteously, and is fair.

Amos, the Prophet warned the leaders about judging unjustly. Listen to the wisdom of the Prophet, "*Ye who turn judgment to wormwood, and leave off righteousness in the earth,*" [Amos 5:7].

When leaders do not judge righteously or continually oppress the poor, are as Henry said in his commentary of [*Amos V7*], "*corruptio optimi pessima*" (Corruption of the best is the worst of all); [**Matthew Henry Bible Commentary Complete, 1712**].

Amos, the Prophet, also warned that one that does wrong under the pretense of doing right is repulsive, hurtful, and is an abomination in the sight of God. We are warned about hypocrisy throughout Scripture, if it makes God ill how much more so should it make us that see it, because we would not dare to be an adherent.

There are consequences to these types of actions if not corrected they will be eternal. Kings cannot allow the poor to be oppressed and has no other voice than his to speak for them.

The woman who a king/leader chooses for a wife must have virtuous qualities; those qualities are of great value.

PART II:

THE PRICE OF A VIRTUOUS WOMAN:
PROVERBS 31:10-14

V10: "Who can find a Virtuous Woman? For her price is far above rubies."

A virtuous woman is well thought of both by the community, her husband, and her children," *A virtuous woman is a crown of her husband: but she that maketh ashamed is a rottenness in his bones,"* [Proverbs 12:4].

When a woman allows these conditions to beset her; works no good toward the family. Spiritual rottenness in a female with these characteristics is defined as a morally offensive, unpleasant, corrupt, miserable, and contentious woman.

Solomon, in his wisdom, reminds us further that finding a wife is a good thing. Listen to what the Preacher wrote, *"Whosoever findeth a wife, findeth a good thing; and obtaineth favour of the Lord,"* [Proverbs 18:22].

A good wife is a woman of wisdom and one of prudence (discretion, farsightedness, practicality, sagacity), *"House and riches are an inheritance of father; and a prudent wife is from the Lord,"* [Proverbs 19:14].

Prudence is the ability to govern and discipline oneself using reason. As well, having sagacity in the management of affairs, which goes along with discipline. Her ability to use skill and good judgment in the uses of their resources moves with caution as to danger or risk to avoid losses.

A woman with good judgment is being farsighted, looking down the road or planning for her family, which includes, her children and their future, *"For the children ought not to lay up for the parents, but the parents for the children,"* [2 Corinthians 12:14c].

A woman who is focused on her family uses realism because she also has the responsibility for her household, not given to fantasizing but rationality in her day-to-day planning for the entire household, She plans for her children's care while they are with her, as well in their future, if ever they have need of assistance.

V11: The heart of her husband doth safely trust in her, so that he shall have no need of spoil."

This verse can be seen as a symbol of a wise woman counseling her son about the woman standing behind her husband; one who he knows is trustworthy because she is a godly woman. She will not waste his resources or neglect her duties; nothing is left unattended. Her husband trusts her because she has shown him through her actions and diligence that she is worthy of his praise of her as a godly and sage wife.

There is posterity in her household. [*Proverbs 31:18*] also references the fact that she does not waste the profits gained from her labour and nor her husband's wealth, *"Her candle goeth not out by night,"* [*Proverbs 31:18b*].

She is, *"A wife of noble character,"* [*Proverbs 3:12:4*].

The Scripture gives Ruth an excellent example. She left her family and country to follow Naomi, her mother-in-law to a better and more enduring life. She placed Naomi's interest above hers, because she was her family and took on the responsibility for getting food for the family by gleaning in the fields just as a wife does for her husband and family.

Her dedication and faithfulness were rewarded with her being in the genealogy of our Lord and Savior Jesus Christ. Boaz, a close family member, observed her faithfulness and dedication to her mother-in-law her reputation untarnished, known in the city of Bethlehem of Judea as such; knew she would be a virtuous wife.

The scripture tells us that he said, *"And now, my daughter, fear not; I will do to thee all that thou requireth: for all the city of people doeth know that thou are a virtuous woman."* [*Ruth 3:11*].

We have a spiritual dictum, *"Older women likewise are to be reverent in behavior, not slanderers or slaves to much wine. They are to teach what is good, and so train the young women to love their husbands and children, to be self-controlled, pure, working at home, kind, and submissive to their own husbands, that the word of God may not be reviled,"* [*Titus 2:3-5*].

She is obedient to the will of God for her life, *"Wives, submit to your own husbands, as to the Lord. For the husband is the head of the wife even as Christ is* the head of the church, His body, and is Himself [Its] Savior. Now as the church submits to Christ, so also wives should submit in everything to their husbands," [Ephesians 5:22-24].

She is Spiritually dressed, "But let your adorning be the hidden person of the heart with the imperishable beauty of a gentle and quiet spirit, which in God's sight is very precious," [I Peter 3:4].

Her Faith is strong in God's promises, "By faith Sarah herself received power to conceive, even when she was past the age, since she considered Him faithful who had promised," [Hebrews 11:11].

Her conduct is that of a godly woman, "Let a woman learn quietly with all submissiveness. I do not permit a woman to teach or to exercise authority over a man; rather, she is to remain quiet. For Adam was formed first, then Eve; and Adam was not deceived, but the woman was deceived and became a transgressor. Yet she will be saved through childbearing—if they continue in faith, love, and holiness, with self-control," [I Timothy 2:11-15].

V12: "She will do him good and not evil all the days of her life."

In the biblical account of Abigail, her husband Nabal, though he had great possessions in the land of Carmel, did not honor King David's request to send food for his men and him.

However, her prudence and farsightedness as a wife temporarily prevented his death at the hands of David, *"Now Abigail made haste, and took two hundred loaves and two bottles of wine and five sheep ready dressed, and five measure of parched corn, and a hundred clusters of raisins, and two hundred cakes of figs, and laid them on the asses. She told not her husband Nabal," [I Samuel 25:18-22]*

In the same biblical account in *[I Samuel 25:26-27]* Abigail prevented her husband from being killed, though he was an evil man, yet as a dutiful wife prudent in her actions, did what was right in the sight of God.

Even though husbands make a misstep at times, it is not good for the wife to compound the problem by adding to his wrong by sitting by and not doing anything, especially if it is within her power. Each person is responsible for their actions whether they are doing right or wrong, God pays us for both, right/good, bad/evil.

A good wife is a gift from God. She attends to her husband's household, which gives him an opportunity and relief when he sits in the gate with the elders of the city. He can feel relief that he has such a valuable gift from God.

Abigail was that gift to her husband Nabal, *"A man's gift maketh room for him, and bringeth him before great men," [Proverbs 18:16]*.

She was prudent enough to give a gift to David, the King and pacified his anger, *"A gift in secret pacifieth anger," [Proverbs 21:14a]*.

V13: "She seeketh wool and flax, and worketh willingly with her hands."

Flax were the fibers used, at that time, to make Linen, *[Ezekiel 44:18]*.

The virtuous wife seeketh indicates her working diligently and willingly with her hands to acquire the necessary items for their clothing for winter and summer.

Seeking wool and flax was necessary. Linen made from flax was acceptable before God. Just as a virtuous wife is acceptable to God. When her husband went into the temple, he had to be dressed appropriately in Linen so as not to sweat which was unacceptable in worship to God.

She was mindful of the command, ensuring her husband had on the proper attire; as were her household for worshipping, "*They shall have linen bonnets upon their heads, and shall have linen breeches upon their loins; they shall not gird themselves with anything that causeth sweat," [Ezekiel 44:18.]*.

Linen was made from fiber and could not be worn to worship God in a combination with other fabrics, "*Thou shalt not wear a garment of divers sorts, as of woollen and linen together," [Deuteronomy 22:11]*.

There were rules for the Priesthood that served before God in the Temple, "*They shall have linen bonnets upon their heads, and shall have linen breeches upon their loins; they shall not gird themselves with anything that causeth sweat," [Ibid]*.

"*And for Aaron's sons thou shalt make coats, and thou shalt make for them girdles, and bonnets shalt thou make for them, for glory and for beauty. And thou shalt put them upon Aaron thy brother, and his sons with him; and shalt anoint them, and consecrate them, and sanctify them, that they may minister unto me in the priest's office. And thou shalt make them linen breeches to cover their nakedness; from the loins even unto the thighs they shall reach," [Ezekiel 28:40–42]*.

"*Ye shall keep my statutes. Thou shalt not let thy cattle gender with a diverse kind: thou shalt not sow thy field with mingled seed: neither shall a garment mingled of linen and woollen come upon thee," [Leviticus 19:19]*.

We also are of the royal priesthood with rules and statues to keep as well. The Proverbial Woman knew and kept these statues for she excelleth.

Peter tells us that, "*But ye are a chosen generation, a royal priesthood, a holy nation, a peculiar people; that ye should shew forth the praises of Him who hath called you out of darkness into His marvelous light," [2 Peter 2:9]*.

V14: She is like the merchant ships; she bringeth her food from afar."

The virtuous wife seeks afar to bring the best for her family even if she must ship it in. We see in Scripture Solomon built ships to bring in Merchandise for afar," *And King Solomon made a navy of ships in Eziongeber, which is beside Eloth, on the shore of the Red Sea, in the land of Edom. And Hiram sent in the navy his servants, shipmen that had knowledge of the sea, with the servants of Solomon. And they came to Ophir, and fetched from thence gold, four hundred and twenty talents, and brought it to King Solomon," [I Kings 9:26-28].*

The woman who cares for her family wants the best for them and will go to whatever length it takes to accomplish it. She purchases food from foreign places in abundance, which is also a blessing. She has many for whom she cares for in her household and in the community, which included, sharing with the poor or less fortunate.

She makes sure her good management brings a profit. She uses every thread of Linen to make garments and with the excess material she makes sashes and sells them to the merchants for profit, *"She makes Linen garments and sells them; she delivers sashes to the merchants,"* [Proverbs 31:24].

The sashes were of fine Linen embroidered in blue, purple, and scarlet. They were part of the Priestly ritual garments. The purpose of the sash was for *"glory and beauty,"* [Ezekiel 28:41].

The garments were worn and desired in Biblical times which bought her a profit for her household.

The resourceful woman in any dispensation of time will make use of all the resources she has at her disposal and not waste her husband money or her additional income.

As a seamstress knows, there is always additional material left after they have cut the materials according to the pattern. Usually there is enough material left for a scarf, belt, sash, or even scraps used to make a quilt.

A virtuous woman cares for her family, those qualities are necessary for a peaceful home and family life.

PART III:
A WOMAN CARES FOR HER FAMILY
PROVERBS 31:15-19

V15: *"She rises also while it is yet night, and giveth meat to her household, and a portion to her maiden."*

She does not let the sun catch her sleeping. This implies finding prey to kill. She is skilled, she has strength that a young woman would have, as well as diligence. Rarely do we find women in Scripture who are skilled at hunting meat. She is also brave pursuing every avenue using every skill to accomplish her goal of providing for her family and entire household, *"Not slothful in business; fervent in spirit; serving the Lord,"* [Romans 12:11].

Physical strength like exercise is necessary, but what is most important is the fact that we are focusing on our Spirituality for this is lasting. Over time our bodies lessen in strength and our abilities to exercise at the rate we did when younger lessen as well, but our spiritual strength can increase, because it is eternal in nature.

Paul reminded Timothy of these facts in a letter to his son in the Gospel, *"For bodily exercise profiteth little: but godliness is profitable unto all things, having promise of the life that now is, and of that which is to come,"* [I Timothy 4:8].

She is a faithful steward in the things of which she has charge. Luke reminds us in this manner, *"And the Lord said, who then is that faithful and wise steward, whom his lord shall make ruler over his household, to give them their portion of meat in due season?"* [Luke 12:42].

The Proverbial Woman is not only a faithful Stewart over her household, but also, she is faithful to God with all the first fruits of her increase. Listen to what Malachi, the Prophet wrote, according to the prophecy given him by God, *"Bring ye all the tithes into the storehouse, that there may be meat in mine house, and prove Me herewith saith the Lord of Host, if I will not open the windows of heaven, and pour you out a blessing, that there shall not be room enough to receive it,"* [Malachi 3:10].

The Psalmist wrote as a reminder that God takes care of His children and those who love, honor, and reverences with fear, His authority over their lives, *"He has given meat unto them that fear Him; He will ever be mindful of His covenant,"* [Psalms 111:5].

The Lord provides for His children; His children also have the responsibility to go out and seek or take advantage of those blessings. Strength, resolve, and stealth is needed in hunting as well as preparing the meat for cooking. She does not wait hours to rise and prepare for the hunt. To get a prey successfully requires you go before the prey begin moving around. Hunting requires cunning or she is first at the market so she can get the choicest of meats, either of these recourses requires diligence.

Listen to the teaching of Job, *"Behold the asses in the desert, go forth to their work, rising betimes for a prey. The wilderness yeildeth food for them and for their children,"* [Job 24:5].

Job expresses further that God is the giver of all things, *"Out of whose womb came the ice? And the hoary frost of heaven who hath gendered it?"* [Job 38:29].

We must go forth to our work of gathering food for our families as the Proverbial Woman did making every minute count. Our addition to the welfare of the family helps our husbands be successful; one person carrying all the burden is difficult. God does His part, keeps His promises, keeps His covenant with His people. We must do our part as well.

She has a spirit of diligence, strength, and uses the mind that God blessed her with to reason, plan, and execute those plans, *"He hath given meat unto them that fear him: He will ever be mindful of His covenant,"* [Psalms 111:5; Ibid].

"And He said unto His disciples, Therefore I say unto you, take no thought for your life, what ye shall eat; neither for the body, what ye shall put on. The life is more than meat, and the body is more than raiment. Consider the ravens: for they neither sow nor reap; which neither have storehouse nor barn; and God feedeth them: how much more are ye better than the fowls? And which of you with taking thought can add to his stature one cubit? If ye then be not able to do that thing which is least, why take ye thought for the rest? Consider the lilies how they grow: they toil not, they spin not; and yet I say unto you, that Solomon in all his glory was not arrayed like one of these. If then God so clothe the grass, which is today in the field, and tomorrow is cast into the oven; how much more will He clothe you, O ye of little faith?" [Luke 12:22-28].

She is never slothful in business or personal duties, *"Not slothful in business; fervent in spirit; serving the Lord,"* [Ibid].

We, like the Proverbial Woman work in His Kingdom, not being slothful, but bear fruit to God that we are pleasing in His sight, *"And now also the axe is laid unto the root of the trees: therefore, every tree which bringeth not forth good fruit is hewn down, and cast into the fire,"* [Matthew 3:10].

V16: "She considereth a field, and buyeth it: with the fruit of her hands, she planeth a vineyard."

It takes resolve and wisdom to make the excess money needed to buy a field for a vineyard. She does not use the household budget for this. We read in *Proverbs 31:14, "She sells sashes to the merchant"* which garners her a profit.

She plants a vineyard with the money she makes. When planting anything the area must be cleared. Rocks were in abundance in those times, they had to be cleared, along with the trees, bushes, weeds, and all other debris. It takes strength and focus to get this done. It is an added expense and task to her already busy day. The vineyard must be cared for and harvested. She and her servants addressed this task because it also brings her family profit.

Listen to what the Prophet Isaiah said, *"And he fenced it, and gathered out the stones thereof, and planted it with choicest vine, and built a tower in the midst of it, and also make a winepress therein: and he looked that it should bring forth grapes, and it bought forth wild grapes," [Isaiah 5:2].*

This gives a vivid picture of what it takes to produce a profit. Also, this is a picture of the people of God, the house of Israel. We today are part of God's vineyard, we are His people, and He cares for His people; His Salvation, Grace, and Mercy helps prune His children that their faithfulness and obedience may become eatable fruit on the vine. Also, the wild grapes indicates that there were people of God who were not obedient as promised.

The virtuous woman here is faithful and lives up to her husband's expectations and her duties.

V17: "She girdeth her loins with strength, and strengtheneth her arms."

This verse is a continuation of [*Proverbs 31:16*]. It takes a bit of strength to clear land. She is strong, not letting herself become weak for the lack of activity. She prepares for the workday in the field; she is mentally prepared for the day. Working strengthens our arms and backs.

She is out front setting the example for all to see.

This verse is also a furtherance of the focus of one woman's tenacity in her duties as a faithful wife and home minister of their lives, *[Isaiah 5:2 Ibid]*.

Moses reminded the people who they belong to and where all blessings come from. We do not, in and of ourselves, have the power to create our blessings. The Proverbial Woman knows from whence comes her blessing as we should as well; all blessings are from God. He is the giver of all things pertaining to life and Salvation we have nothing we can give God to requite His mercy toward us, *"Do ye thus requite the Lord, O foolish people and unwise? is not He thy Father that hath bought thee? hath He not made thee, and established thee?"* [*Deuteronomy 32:6*].

Luke encourages us in this manner, *"Let your loins be girded about and your light burning,"* [*Luke 12:35*].

Paul tells us, *"Finally, my brethren; be strong in the Lord, and in the power of His might,"* [*Ephesians 6:10*].

We can do all thing if we depend upon our Father, *"Our strength comes from the Lord who made heaven and earth,"* [*Ibid*].

The Prophet Ezra reminds us to, *"Look to the Lord and His strength; seek His face always,"* I *Chronicles 16:11*].

This statement can be thought of in a Spiritual sense as well as it takes strength and resolve to continue to work in the vineyard and not be guilty of disobedience as Israel was at one time. They continually break their promises to God – God does not break His promises to man; however, there is an "If" condition there, *"If you love me."* God keeps His promises and expects us to keep ours. It is a commandment.

V18: She preceiveth that her merchandise is good: her candle goeth not out by night."

We must always be well-prepared; twenty-four hours a day (or from sun to sun). Jesus gave us a parable of the ten virgins, five wise and five unwise, *"They that were foolish took their lamps and no oil with them,"* [Matthew 25:3].

This parable speaks to the lack of proper preparation for the unexpected and the future. The proverbial woman worked until the task was complete. She did not leave necessary tasks that would ensure her family's future undone. She worked day and night to secure her family's future, always planning for tomorrow or the eventualities in life, because we, if we live long enough, will have unexpected things happen, therefore, we use our wisdom to plan for those times.

Solomon used the example of the wisdom of the ant. One of the smallest of God's creations Solomon tells us, *"Go to the ant, thou sluggard; consider her ways, and be wise,"* [Proverbs 6:6].

Job further reminds us of the wisdom of preparing in this way, *"But ask now the beasts, and they shall teach thee; and the fowls of the air, and they shall tell thee,"* [Job 12:7-8].

We see the beast of the field and the birds of the air hunt and search for their food for their young and themselves. They use their stealth and abilities that God gives them for survival. They are cunning in their pursuit of their prey that they make their efforts count because they know from instinct their young's survival and their survival depends on them.

Humans are the highest animal in God's Kingdom and given the mind to think and reason; if the animals hunt and prepare for their families, how much more so should man who can think and use his wisdom prepare for their families and not let their candle go out by night?

Paul tells us through his God given wisdom how not to be a burden to anyone, *"For yourselves know how ye ought to follow us: for we behaved not ourselves disorderly among you; neither did we eat any man's bread for nought; but wrought with labour and travail night and day, that we might not be chargeable to any of you: not because we have not power, but to make ourselves an ensample unto you to follow us,"* [2 Thessalonians 3:7-9].

The proverbial woman is an example to all who are around her, especially to her household. A woman of God will be about the work of her household because her husband, children, maids, and other servants depend on her.

Her idleness would bring disaster to her family and wishing or worrying about what she did not have for lack of preparation would not produce positive results. David reminds us that, "*It is vain to rise up early, sit up late, to eat the bread of idleness (sorrow) for so He giveth His beloved sleep,*" [Psalms 127:2].

We can have peace and rest when we know that all preparation as much as humanly possible have been made. The arduous work of the righteous gives them blessing of dividends from the Lord. He provides His children rest and sleep. He blesses their efforts and allow them to rest.

So many wrests leading to sorrow because they do not prepare for the night.

This idea of night is not necessarily in darkness, but those lean times we all face in life. Simply because everyday we live on earth is not going to be in abundance according to our desires. Disasters happens in life, sickness, and a mirid of unforeseen incidences, so preparation is necessary, both mental, emotional, and material.

The example of the five unwise virgins only took enough oil for an abbreviated period-of-time, not enough to last if the night persisted or the bridegroom was delayed.

In this light, she served God all of her life, not just a short time during her lifetime. We, like she, must continually eat of the bread from the spiritual table [His Word] and keep the oil of the Word of God ever before us that our vision and faithful be never dimmed. God's word was the light and the bread of life for the people of God in Moses time as [It] was for the Proverbial Woman and as [It] is for the people of God in this dispensation of time.

The Proverbial Woman was faithful; being the example of that faithfulness and service to God her light brightly shining regardless of the trials and tribulations faced in this training ground.

Moses instructed the Priest according to God's Word in the twenty-fourth chapter of Leviticus concerning keeping the lamps of the Tabernacle burning continually, "*Then the Lord spoke to Moses, saying: "Command the children of Israel that they bring to you pure oil of pressed olives for the light, to make the lamps burn continually. Outside the veil of the Testimony, in the tabernacle of meeting, Aaron shall be in charge of it from evening until morning before the Lord continually; it shall be a statute forever in your generations. He shall be in charge of the lamps on the pure gold lampstand before the Lord continually,"* [Leviticus 24:1-4].

Moses instructed them concerning the bread that was to be on the table of the Tabernacle continually, *"And you shall take fine flour and bake twelve cakes with it. Two-tenths of an ephah shall be in each cake. You shall set them in two rows, six in a row, on the pure gold table before the Lord. And you shall put pure frankincense on each row, that it may be on the bread for a memorial, an offering made by fire to the Lord. Every Sabbath he shall set it in order before the Lord continually, being taken from the children of Israel by an everlasting covenant. And it shall be for Aaron and his sons, and they shall eat it in a holy place; for it is most holy to him from the offerings of the* LORD *made by fire, by a perpetual statute,"* [Leviticus 24: 5-9].

The Proverbial Woman kept her light shining in all that she did to serve God as we must. The Psalmist tells us that God is our fountain of life, and He is light and without that light we would not be able to see, *"For with You is the fountain of life; in your light do we see light,"* [Psalms 36:9].

Isaiah tells us to, *"Arise, shine, for your light has come, and the glory of the Lord has risen upon you,"* [Isaiah 60:1].

Paul warns, *"For this reason is says, "Awake, sleeper, and arise from the dead, and Christ will shine on you,"* [Ephesians 5:14].

We like the Proverbial Woman are to keep our light shining not letting our candle go out and keep our lamps filled with oil in our service to God. We cannot allow our lamps to get dim in our service to God as Moses instructed the Priest to keep the lamp burning.

We are ambassadors for Christ living a life of obedience for all to see and not hide our light.

Luke recorded, when Paul and Barnabas were teaching on the Synagogue in Antioch they grew bold after much dispute of their message by the Jews and their lack of appreciation for the message of Salvation said, *"Then Paul and Barnabas waxed bold, and said, It was necessary that the Word of God should first have been spoken to you: but seeing ye put it from you, and judge yourselves unworthy of everlasting life, lo, we turn to the Gentiles. For so hath the Lord commanded us, saying, I have set thee to be a light of the Gentiles, that thou shouldest be for salvation unto the ends of the earth. And when the Gentiles heard this, they were glad, and glorified the Word of the Lord: and as many as were ordained to eternal life believed,"* [Acts 13:46–48].

The people of God are still lights (examples) to the world and the people around them as was the Proverbial Woman. She continually kept her light burning in all things pertaining to her life and her duties and services to God.

The people of God lantern still shine, though we face dark times, the blessing continue to come without fail because of His promise to His children. Night may come, but what she does speaks for her planning shines like a candle in the dark.

The Proverbial Woman expected night (challenging times) would come as well as summer and winter (both grim times) in life but prepared for them. She knew her God would not desert her in times of plenty or times of despair; but looked always to the dawning of spring and fall of life (good times and times of plenty).

Our work on earth is never done day or night it is continual service in faithful to God until we are called home.

V19: *She layeth her hands to the spindle, and her hand holds the distaff."*

The spindle and the distaff were for making thread into yarn – yarn makes cloth, *"And, all the women that were wise hearted did spin with their hands, and brought that which they had spun, both of blue, and of purple, and of scarlet, and of fine linen. And all the women whose heart stirred them up in wisdom spun goats' hair. Not because we have not power, but to make ourselves an ensample unto you to follow us," [Exodus 35:25-26].*

The woman of wisdom uses her skills that God has blessed her with to design, create, the threads she spun into yarn. She works willingly and diligently with her hands to create the merchandise she sells as well to make the linen garments commanded for worship before God, *[ibid]*.

As the example was given to us by Moses, the women then, as did the proverbial woman, was an example of wisdom willingly diligently working with their hands not because they did not have power or could not have their maiden to do it for them, but they, regardless of their status were willing to lead the way as we see in the chapter of the Proverbial Woman.

We in our dispensation of time, are also commanded to teach by example, *"That they may teach the young women to be sober, to love their husbands, to love their children," [Titus 2:4].*

The Proverbial Woman also bought her children up in the admonition and nurture of the Lord and was an example to her sons and daughters, as we must be when raising our children as Paul reminds us, *"And, ye fathers, provoke not your children to wrath: but bring them up in the nurture and admonition of the Lord," [Ephesians 6:4].*

Also, she has the understanding and the expertise to teach her maidens the art of the spindle and distaff. All efforts benefit the family's prosperity for the future.

Staff and Spindle makes the thread and twist into yarn – today we buy our thread from stores. It required patience, diligence, and dedication to make clothes. How more so blessed are we who through the advancements of this modern technological age works less at manual labor, which gives us more time to devote in service to God, as well to aid our fellowman, who is less fortunate.

A Virtuous woman not only cares for her family; but is not selfish; she cares for others around her. She is willing to share her blessings.

PART IV:

THE VIRTUOUS WOMAN HELPS THE NEEDY
PROVERBS 31:20-25

V20: *She stretcheth out her hand to the poor; yes, she reacheth forth her hands to the needy."*

The Preacher tells us, "*He that hath a bountiful eye shall be blessed; for he giveth of his bread to the poor," [Proverbs 22:9].*

The Apostle Paul says it in this way, "*But to do good and to communicate forget not: for such sacrifices God is well pleased," [Hebrews 13:16].*

Solomon reminds us yet again that, *"A virtuous woman is a crown to her husband: but she that maketh ashamed is as rottenness in his bones," [Proverbs 12:4].* Moses reminds us that, "*For the poor shall never cease out of the land; therefore, I command thee, say, thou shalt open thine hand wide unto thy brother, to thy poor, and to the needy, in the land," [Deuteronomy 15:11].*

Paul also reminds us that God is well pleased with our working hard that we might have to give those who need. We know there are always those who cannot work because of situations in their lives whether it be lack of skills, physical, emotional, or not enough resources to survive on from day to day, *"Let him that stole steal no more: but rather let him labour, working with his hands the thing, which is good, that he may have to give to him that needeth," [Ephesians 4:28].*

Though the Proverbial Woman did well, she did not forget the poor and needy, blessing them with a portion of the blessings God had given her.

The Proverbial Woman set the example for her household and the community that working hard is acceptable to God. Her family and servants had no reason to steal, she provides for their needs as well as helping those in her community.

Her actions are speaking louder than any words she could speak. People see and remember – not hear and remember; also, they will remember how you made them feel. The poor and disadvantaged are also important to God; they were then, and they are now.

Jesus reminds us that, "*The poor you will always have, but Me you will not always," [Matthew 26:11].*

It is wise to be adherents of these characteristics we see in the Proverbial Woman.

David tells us God is concerned about and for the poor, "*He hath dispersed, He hath given to the poor; His righteousness endureth forever; His horn shall be exalted with honour*" *[Psalms 112:9]*.

Jesus said, "*Whosoever shall give to drink unto one of the little ones a cup of cold water only in the name of a disciple; he shall in no wise lose his reward,*"*[Matthew 10:42]*.

God blesses our efforts to help the poor and less fortunate.

We cannot always know when it will be our time of need or for a reason unknown to us, we come to be one of the poor or needy, or it could be our children or other loved ones.

Our blessing comes when we help those less fortunate and the needy in their distress and times of urgent needs are wise when we, "*Cast your bread upon the water: for thou shalt find it after many days. Give a portion to seven, and also to eight; for thou knowest not what evil shall be upon the earth,*" *[Ecclesiastes 112:1-2]*.

Solomon also tells us that, "*He that hath pity upon the poor lendeth to the Lord and that which he hath given will He pays again,*" *[Proverbs 19:17]*.

God never fails to bless those who are willing to help the poor. Those who lend to the Lord has no doubt He pays as promised not necessarily in the way that we blessed the poor, but the repayment from God is always above what we think or do.

We see the example of Job showing hospitality to all and refused none, "*If I have put my trust in gold or said to pure gold, 'You are my security,' if I have rejoiced over my great wealth, the fortune my hands had gained, if I have regarded the sun in its radiance or the moon moving in splendor, so that my heart was secretly enticed and my hand offered them a kiss of homage, then these also would be sins to be judged, for I would have been unfaithful to God on high. "If I have rejoiced at my enemy's misfortune or gloated over the trouble that came to him-I have not allowed my mouth to sin by invoking a curse against their life-if those of my household have never said, 'Who has not been filled with Job's meat?'-but no stranger had to spend the night in the street, for my door was always open to the traveler,*" *[Job 31:24-32]*.

V21: *She is not afraid of the snow for her household: for all her household are clothed with Scarlet.*"

She provides the best for everyone. The word Scarlet originated from the Old French scarlet (type of cloth) from the medieval Latin word (Scartatum: Scarlet Cloth) and Persian word is (Saqerlot) a woolen cloth, of certain origin: (http://www.Dictionary.com).

Scarlet has the indication of both purity and sinful acts (results of) in Scripture. We know that the Proverbial Woman was righteous; the reference here is purity. Scarlet is a deep reddish orange color. Wool is reference to purity as well.

"Come let us reason together says the Lord: though your sins be as scarlet, they shall be as white as snow; though they be red like crimson, they shall be as wool," [Isaiah 1:18].

The proverbial woman makes sure all her household is kept warm with the proper clothing which helps maintain their health in the brutal cold of the winter.

As well, she provides clothing for those around her; she is righteous and obedient to the will of God, as she has set the example. Though tough times may come; they are prepared to get through them by faith, as well, she has prepared for both spiritual and physical droughts that may come their way.

We in this day and time, it is also necessary to prepare for the physical and spiritual draughts that will come into our lives. We guide our homes in service to God, as well, can be seen by our Savior as being clothed with Scarlet (purity) as is the example of the Proverbial Woman. We are reminded by Joshua, who knew it is wise, that he and his house would serve God, "*And if it seem evil unto you to serve the Lord, choose you this day whom ye will serve; whether the gods which your fathers served that were on the other side of the flood, or the gods of the Amorites, in whose land ye dwell: but as for me and my house, we will serve the Lord," [Joshua 24:15].*

The world and its attractions can become like the gods of the Amorites in our life as well. Choosing to enjoy the pleasures of the world or depend on the material things of this world is not a wise choice for us now no more than it was for the people of God at that time.

If we chose the world over God, it is the evil; choosing God over the world that is the wisdom.

V22: She maketh herself covering of Tapestry; her clothing is silk and purple."

She maintains the home making it comfortable for her husband after he returned home after a day of sitting in the council with the other elders making important decisions for all the people.

She makes the home atmosphere pleasing and inviting for her husband after he spends a long time away. He knows he is welcome; the meal is prepared, it is comfortable; he finds contentment in the presence of his wife and family because she is a dutiful home minister. He does not arrive to disorder, bickering, discord, but unity, love, and kindness. She speaks to him in a loving and respectful manner. She sets the example for her children, her maidens, and other workers, so they may know how to conduct themselves. She has a good name in the community, her husband is pleased at her and with her.

Also, she dresses in the manner that befits a woman of her status, as well, sets the example for all her household to dress. She sends her husband out each day dressed appropriately for his day among his peers.

He looks as if he has a wife who cares about him.

Her clothing is silk and purple, an indication of the finest.

This verse also gives a picture of the quality of the character of the Proverbial Woman. She was not only well-dressed physically but well-dressed spiritually. We give God our best, be our best in behavior, examples as wives, mothers, neighbors, friends, and daughters. As well her husband was an elder and known in the gates, she could not be an embarrassment to him, with her lack of care in appearance or mannerism. She cared for her physical and spiritual appearance as the people of God should today as well.

> ➢ **We are faithful women of God, and we are part of the royal priesthood; should we not look and conduct ourselves in like manner?**

Though Tapestry, linen, silk, and purple was associated with women and men of questionable character here it associated with the finer quality of life. She imported Linen from afar. Egypt is known for its fine Linen, *"Fine linen with broidered work from Egypt was that which thou spreadest forth to be thy sail; blue and purple from the isles of Elishah was that which covered thee,"* [Ezekiel 27:7].

83

As discussed before Linen was necessary in the presence of God so that there would be no body sweat, *"And thou shalt make them linen breeches to cover their nakedness; from the loins even unto the thighs they shall reach, and:*

The dress of the priesthood that was commanded to appear before God, *"And they shall be upon Aaron, and upon his sons, when they come in unto the tabernacle of the congregation, or when they come near unto the altar to minister in the holy place; that they bear not iniquity and die: it shall be a statute forever unto him and his seed after him,"* [Ezekiel 28:42-43].

Reference to purity when Pharoah honors Joseph, *"And Pharaoh took off his ring from his hand, and put it upon Joseph's hand, and arrayed him in vestures of fine linen, and put a gold chain about his neck,"* [Genesis 41:42].

V23: Her husband is known in the gates, when he sitteth among the elders of the land."

Think how pleased he feels when sitting among other elders. He knows his wife is doing him good and her reputation is unchallengeable. She is faithful in all things to her family and The God of Heaven, *"A virtuous woman is a crown to her husband: but she that maketh ashamed is as rottenness in his bones," [Proverbs 12:4].*

She is the glory of her husband, *"For a man indeed ought not to cover his head, forasmuch as he is the image and glory of God: but the woman is the glory of the man,"* [I Corinthians 11:7].

"And the Lord God formed man of the dust of the ground and breathed into his nostrils the breath of life; and man became a living soul," [Genesis 2:7].

(Then God made woman from the rib of the man, and she became a living soul).

He sits with men of wisdom in the city, because he is considered as wise; when he speaks, he is known for his wisdom, *"Wisdom is too high for a fool: he openeth not his mouth in the gate," [Proverbs 24:7].*

Important and knowledgeable people oversaw legal and commercial business.

As we have our city leaders today, so the Elders of the city were then. Her husband had to be confident that his home was being taken care of as well, so that he could assist successfully, in directing the affairs of the city, and caring for the overall population there of which they had charge, *"And when he that doth flee unto one of those cities shall stand at the entering of the gate of the city and shall declare his cause in the ears of the elders of that city, they shall take him into the city unto them, and give him a place, that he may dwell among them," [Joshua 20:4].*

Women whose husbands are leaders in a city or has the responsibility of the public safety or care in any way, are to be as responsible at home as he is in the public. His reputation as a husband must be acceptable in the manner so approved by God.

It matters the appearance and the reputation of the leaders' wives; she excelled in this as well.

The Book of Ruth, wife of Boaz, one of the Elders of Bethlehem of Judea, gives us an example of a woman of exemplary character and praised by all the Elders of the city and purchased by Boaz because of her exemplary character, love, faithfulness to God, and care for her mother-in-law Naomi, *"Then went Boaz up to the gate, and sat him down there: and, behold, the kinsman of whom Boaz spake came by; unto whom he said, Ho, such a one! turn aside, sit down here, and he turned aside and sat down," [Ruth 4:1].*

"Moreover, Ruth the Moabitess, the wife of Mahlon, have I purchased to be my wife, to raise up the name of the dead upon his inheritance, that the name of the dead be not cut off from among his brethren, and from the gate of his place: ye are witnesses this day. And all the people that were in the gate, and the elders, said, we are witnesses. The Lord makes the woman that is come into thine house like Rachel and like Leah, which two did build the house of Israel: and do thou worthily in Ephratah and be famous in Bethlehem: And let thy house be like the house of Pharez, whom Tamar bare unto Judah, of the seed which the Lord shall give thee of this young woman," [Ruth 4:10-12].

Ruth was a treasure to the household of Boaz; he considered her a precious jewel from God; one who would do him good and not evil all the days of his life. She gleaned in his fields, and he found her to be righteous and loved God and worshipped Him in in truth and in spirit.

Ruth is in the genealogy of our Lord and Savior Jesus Christ, because she like the Proverbial Woman excelled. God blessed her because of her love and faithfulness.

The Elder sits speaking with wisdom concerning the issues of the people with the knowledge that his wife is attending to her duties at home and not out being a busy body in other men matters or talking about what she does or what they have. She is too resolute and busy with her family life and aiding others to participate in useless (vain) conversation.

V24: "She maketh fine linen, and selleth it, and delivereth girdles unto the merchants."

She sells everything necessary for clothing and proper dress from the undergarments to the very belts and sashes, which were all part of dress then; it equals our intimate lingerie, slips, outer garments, and belts in this dispensation of time.

We see from Scripture she only sells and makes the best; she does not give clothing items made of a lesser quality of materials, but uses the best, Linen, *"Syria was thy merchant by reason of the multitude of the wares of thy making: they occupied in thy fairs with emeralds, purple, and broidered work, and fine linen, and coral, and agate,"* [Ezekiel 27:16].

Lydia, like the Proverbial woman, a merchant, was a seller of purple, *"And a certain woman named Lydia, a seller of purple, of the city of Thyatira, which worshipped God, heard us: whose heart the Lord opened, that she attended unto the things which were spoken of Paul.*

And when she was baptized, and her household, she besought us, saying, If ye have judged me to be faithful to the Lord, come into my house, and abide there. And she constrained us," [Acts 16:14-15].

The Proverbial Woman did not leave any steps incomplete. When she sold to the merchants, they of course would want a full garment to sell their customers. She was seen as a dependable supplier, as well.

She is what is known as a modern-day entrepreneur (capitalist). There are many Lydia and Proverbial Women today that are businesswomen conducting business to assist their families and add to the incomes of their households.

V25: "Strength and honor are her clothing; and she shall rejoice in time to come."

Her constant work and diligence, she wears like a garment, which brings her honor. Her honor comes in time as she fulfills and will fulfill her duties until she cannot any longer. She passes these talents to her sons and daughter; she is pleased as time passes with her accomplishments and her children and husband honor her in her later years.

As her resolve and willingness were to be obedient and pleasing to God, she is deserving of the honor bestowed upon her. As her clothing of faithfulness and duty fits well, so does the honor she has as a faithful wife, mother, and servants of God.

There is no doubt in her husband's view that she is deserving of the honor, *"The fear of the Lord prolongeth days: but the years of the wicked shall be shortened,"* [Proverbs 10:27].

Like the good name chosen rather than riches, she will be remembered as one who extended her hand to the poor and needy and one manner or the other provided aid for those within her preview of influence. People will remember her kindness and compassion for the poor and those she helped will speak of her good deeds often. For she always considered the grace of God a better and more enduring reward, *"The memory of the just is blessed; but the name of the wicked shall rot,"* [Proverbs 10:7].

"The glory of young men is their strength, and the beauty of old man is their gray head," [Proverbs 20:29].

The Scripture here compare strength and honor using the simile (like) gray headed; it is considered a sign of wisdom if it is found among the righteous, *"The hoary head is a crown of glory, if it be found in the way of righteousness,"* [Proverbs 16:31].

Later in life, as the years wain away, and her hair becomes gray, and her strength diminishes as Solomon wrote in the Twelfth Chapter of the Book of Ecclesiastes, she can look back and know that she did all that she could while it was day, her years and strength were spent in the service of God, taking care of the responsibilities of her household, and ever striving to be a godly woman.

Her husband and children will recall all her efforts throughout their lives and the provisions she as a mother and wife made for her family, caring for them as well as others less fortunate in the community. By keeping herself unspotted from the world she was the example to them while she was young and now she is older, has even more honor because, of her faithfulness and love.

The Proverbial Woman is respectful of her husband and his authority and position in the home as well as an Elder, *"Thou shall rise up before the hoary head, and honor the face of the old man, and fear thy God, I am The Lord," [Leviticus 19:32].*

> ➤ **How can we teach our children and future generations the respect they should have for their elders regardless of who they are, if we do not know how to conduct ourselves in their presence or respond in the right manner to a request?**

Respect for elders is not just an Old Testament dictum but is a universal one. The Proverbial Woman would receive the respect she is due because she taught her children how to respect elders and she lived the example before them showing respect for her husband their father, and (their servant's master), so she taught her children to, *"Honor they Father and they Mother that thy days may be long in the land which the Lord thy God giveth thee," [Exodus 20:12].*

"For God commanded, saying, Honour thy father and mother: and He that curseth father or mother, let him die the death," [Matthew 15:4].

Life eternal is within the righteousness of God. Wisdom is the key to life on earth and for an eternity, *"In the way of the righteousness is life: and in the pathway thereof is no death," [Proverbs 12:28].*

God requires of parents that they raise their children to respect and honor their elders; however, if our children or younger women do not see us honoring the elders or our husbands, we cannot expect that they will know how to respect or honor their parents, the elders, or their husbands as God commands.

That wisdom that is pleasing to God comes from God. We gain strength and honor from the wisdom of God, it is perfect and without fault and we will know that we are pleasing to Him if we are walking in the manner He so desire for His children, *"Every good gift and every perfect gift is from above, and cometh down from the Father of lights, with whom is no variableness, neither shadow of turning," [James 1:17].*

The virtuous woman is humble, kind, understanding, peaceable, and engenders (promotes) peace, and her tongue is the law of kindness.

PART V:

THE VIRTUOUS WOMAN SPEAKS WISDOM
PROVERBS 31:26-31

V26: "She openeth her mouth with wisdom; and in her tongue is the law of kindness."

Experience brings wisdom, faithfulness to God, also, so do prayer and meditation bring wisdom. When she speaks it should be through kindness in an acceptable tone that entreats the listener without being harsh. Kindness is one of the Fruit of the Spirit, *"But the fruit of the Spirit is love, joy, peace, longsuffering, gentleness, goodness, faith, Meekness, and temperance: against such there is no law,"* [Galatians 5:22-23].

"Follow peace with all yea and holiness, without which no man shall see the Lord: Looking diligently lest any man fail of the grace of God; lest any root of bitterness springing up trouble you, and thereby many be defiled. Lest there be any fornicator or profane person, as Esau, who for one morsel of meat sold his birthright. For ye know how that afterward when he would have inherited the blessing, he was rejected: for he found no place of repentance, though he sought it carefully with tears," [Hebrews 12:14-17].

With her tongue she does not cause confusion, private or public, she encourages peace not confusion, *"Even so the tongue is a little member, and boasteth great things. Behold, how great a matter a little fire kindleth, and the tongue is a fire, a world of iniquity: so is the tongue among our members, that it defileth the whole body, and setteth on fire the course of nature; and it is set on fire of hell. For every kind of beasts, and of birds, and of serpents, and of things in the sea, is tamed, and hath been tamed of mankind: But the tongue can no man tame; it is an unruly evil, full of deadly poison,"* [James 3:5-8].

She thinks well, therefore she speaks well; out of the issues of the heart the mouth speaks. If we harbor bitterness, resentment, and all negative things in our minds (hearts) we can but act the way and speak the way we are thinking, *"Keep thy heart with all diligence; for out of it are the issues of life,"* [Proverbs 4:23].

Sweet and bitter water cannot flow from the same fountain, *"Doth a fountain sends forth at the same place sweet water and bitter? Can the fig tree, my brethren, bear olive berries? either a vine, figs? so can no fountain both yield salt water and fresh. Who is a wise man and endued with knowledge among you? let him shew out of a good conversation his works with meekness of wisdom,"* [James 3:11-13].

There is an acceptable way to say anything that is more welcoming to the listening ear than the words that are harsh and unkind, *"Let your speech be always with grace, seasoned with salt, that ye may know how ye ought to answer every man, "[Colossians 4:6]."*

We are known by our fruits.

The Proverbial Woman grew in grace and knowledge, which is pleasing to God as we must grow in the grace and knowledge of Jesus Christ, *"But grow in grace, and in the knowledge,"* [2 Peter 3:18].

As well, desiring the sincere milk of the work, without which a Christian cannot grow whether it was during the Proverbial Woman lifetime or ours, *"As newborn babes, desire the sincere milk of the word, that ye may grow thereby,"[I Peter 2:2].*

Also, Mercy and goodness are shown to be desired, *"The desire of a man is his kindness: and a poor man is better than a liar,"* [Proverbs 19:22].

The Proverbial Woman was praised for her kindness and so will we be. God shows us mercy (kindness) we can do no less; *"And shewing mercy unto thousands of them that love Me, and keep My commandments,"* [Exodus 20:6].

Genesis to Revelations we see the kindness, mercy, and faithfulness of God without cease, *"Know therefore, that the Lord thy God, He is God, the faithful God, which keepeth covenant and mercy with them that love Him and keep His commandments to a thousand generations,"* [Deuteronomy 7:9].

We should pursue goodness and mercy as did the Proverbial Woman, *"Surely goodness and mercy shall follow me all the days of my life: and I will dwell in the house of the Lord forever,"* [Psalms 23:6].

We draw others with kindness, as did the Proverbial Woman. Listen at the Prophet Jeremiah's message to the people from God, *"The Lord hath appeared of old unto me, saying, Yea, I have loved thee with an everlasting love: therefore, with lovingkindness have I drawn thee,"* [Jeremiah 31:3].

God is the Lord, and He draws us. Drawing means pulling toward, *"And I, if I be lifted up from the earth, will draw all men unto Me,"* [John 12:32].

"The fear of the Lord tendeth to life; and he that hath it shall abide satisfied; he shall not be visited with evil," [Proverbs 19:23].

"Draw near to God, and He will draw near you," [James 4:8a].

Pious and edifying speech is the product of a good heart, "The tree is known by its fruit," *"Either make the tree good, and his fruit good; or else make the tree corrupt, and his fruit corrupt: for the tree is known by his fruit," [Matthew 12:33].*

"A wholesome tongue is a tree of life: but perverseness therein is a breach in the spirit," [Proverbs 15:4].

"The lips of the wise disperse knowledge: but the heart of the foolish doeth not so," [Proverbs 15:7].

"A wrathful man stirreth up strife: but he that is slow to anger appeaseth

strife," [Proverbs 15:18].

"Put on then, as God's chosen ones, holy and beloved, compassionate hearts, kindness, humility, meekness, and patience," [Colossians 3:12].

Solomon admonishes that, *"A man who is kind benefits himself, but a cruel man hurts himself," [Proverbs 11:17].*

Also, he reminds us that, *"He that soweth iniquity shall reap vanity: and the rod of his anger shall fail," [Proverbs 22:8].*

Paul in one of his letters to the Ephesians admonishes us in the way that we communicate should be in this manner, *"Let no corrupt communication proceed out of your mouth, but that which is good to the use of edifying, that it may minister grace unto the hearers," [Ephesians 4:29].*

The same warning in the Old Testament we find in the New Testament, *"Do not be deceived: God is not mocked, for whatever one sows, that will he also reap," [Galatians 6:7].*

The Proverbial Woman, because she has authority, is not overbearing or oppressive with her words. She does not supervise with a prideful spirit, but in a humble and kind manner.

Then again, authority one has does not entitle them to be inconsiderate of those they supervise.

Soft answers turn away wrath and ensures peace, *"A soft answer turneth away wrath: but grievous words stir up anger. The tongue of the wise useth knowledge aright: but the mouth of fools poureth out foolishness," [Proverbs 15:1-5].*

Paul tells us, *"With all lowliness and meekness, with longsuffering, forbearing one another in love,"* [Ephesians 4:2].

The Proverbial Woman was person of noble character. She condescended to keep peace in her family though she was wealthy and had the authority over her household. She through the kindness and willingness, knew how to keep peace and manage any difference (strife) between her servants.

Abraham was a person of noble character; he to knew how to humble himself to a lower estate through he was the elder in his family and a greater man than Lot his brother. He was a mild-mannered man and chose to allow others to go first and he took the last position, *"And there was a strife between the herdsmen of Abram's cattle and the herdsmen of Lot's cattle: and the Canaanite and the Perizzite dwelled then in the land. And Abram said unto Lot, let there be no strife, I pray thee, between me and thee, and between my herdsmen and thy herdsmen; for we be brethren. Is not the whole land before thee? separate thyself, I pray thee, from me: if thou wilt take the left hand, then I will go to the right; or if thou depart to the right hand, then I will go to the left,"* [Genesis 13:7-9].

It is inevitable that when humans dwell together there will be strife. But those who live by and pursue peace will keep peace and thereby have peace.

As Scripture reminds us, Abraham knew God as Jehovah-Jireh (God will provide). The Proverbial Woman also knew the God she served would provide, but she also knew she must make the effort to take advantage of the blessings provided.

Kindness goes a mile in effectiveness when unkindness only goes a foot. Servants at that time, as now, have rights like every other human poor or rich. The Proverbial Woman's wisdom was a constant reminder that God is overall.

Kindness is one of the many attributes of love. When we are kind to others we are blessed and enjoy the fruits of our efforts, *"Death and life are in the power of the tongue: and they that love it shall eat the fruit thereof,"* [Proverbs 18:21].

Solomon says this of Wisdom, *"Happy is the man that findeth wisdom, and the man that getteth understanding. For the merchandise of it is better than the merchandise of silver, and the gain thereof than fine gold. She is more precious than rubies: and all the things thou canst desire are not to be compared unto her. Length of days is in her right hand, and in her left-hand riches and honour. Her ways are ways of pleasantness, and all her paths are peace. She is a tree of life to them that lay hold upon her: and happy is everyone that retaineth her,"* [Proverbs 3:13-18].

And further, *"The wise shall inherit glory: but shame shall be the promotion of fools,"* [Proverbs 3:35].

Wisdom takes humility and obedience. Wisdom demands that we be clothed in the Word of God. Listen at what David said, *"The steps of a good man are ordered by the Lord,"* [Psalms 37:23].

Paul tells us that we should be willing to forebear with our fellowman, *With all lowliness and meekness, with longsuffering, forbearing one another in love,"* [Ephesians 3:2].

Our mouths are for speaking those words which edify and build up, *"The mouth of the righteous speaketh wisdom, and his tongue talketh of judgment,"* [Proverbs 37:30].

Listen at the wisdom that God taught Job:

➤ **"Can a man darken the council of God?"** [Job 38:2].
➤ **Is this not provoking our Heavenly Father?**
➤ **Do we know more than God?** [Job 38:2].
➤ **"Hast, thou commanded the morning since thy days; and caused the dayspring to know his place?** [Job 38:12].

Job spoke of man's weakness before the Almighty God. The thirty-nineth chapter of the Book of Job expresses the limits of man and use of powerful animals to express sin and its fatal consequences. It is folly and lack of wisdom blinded by sin to think we can escape the wrath of God in our disobedience, [Job 39:1-30].

Wisdom begins with the Lord.

Sisters when our ways are not pleasing to God, all our trying will be bought too naught. We have the same duties and responsibilities listed in Scripture to perform if we want to get the same praise as the Proverbial Woman; and to be pleasing to God, we must have the same humble obedient spirit.

We cannot allow all that we do to become vanity in God's sight.

Vanity is an earthly maneuver from the toolbox of Satan. The deep pits of the world are still there and are laden with temptation, lust, evil desires, intent, and betrayal. We must, as mothers, continue to train and teach.

James asked and answered, *"Who is wise and endued with knowledge among you? Let him shew out of a good conversation his work with meekness and wisdom,"* *[James 3:13].*

Solomon compared/contrasted the difference in pleasant and unpleasant speaking, *"There is that speaketh like the piercing of a sword: but the tongue of the wise is health,"* *[Proverbs 12:8].*

And *"The tongue of the wise useth knowledge aright,"* *[Proverbs 15:2a].*

Jesus in his interaction with the Pharisees because he knew their hearts were evil, did not speak what was right nor out of kindness said, *"Make a tree good and its fruit will be good or make a tree bad and its fruit will be bad, for a tree is recognized by its fruit. You brood of vipers, how can you who are evil say anything good? For the mouth speaks what the heart is full of. A good man brings good things out of the good stored up in him, and an evil man brings evil things out of the evil stored up in him. But I tell you that everyone will have to give account on the day of judgment for every empty word they have spoken. For by your words, you will be acquitted, and by your words you will be condemned, "[Matthew 12:33-37].*

Christians cannot be churlish (rude, boorish, impolite) or mean-spirited towards others or the less fortunate. The Proverbial Woman attitudes and actions toward others were described in this way, *"Her tongue was the law of kindness,"* *[Proverbs 31:26b].*

She set the standards with her speech and how she interacted with and spoke to others around her. I am sure she had stressful days, long days, at times unsuccessful day, we all do; but note she never allowed herself to be pulled so far into allowing the temporal events taking place around her to push her into being unkind. It is hard to maintain our composures at times, but if we stop take a moment to think before we speak, or act will not fall into error before God.

> ➢ **Do we always manage life and it stresses with composure?**

V27: She looketh well to the ways of her household, and eateth not the bread of idleness."

Preparing for all seasons is a mark of wisdom, idleness bring want, and want poverty, *"A slack hand causes poverty, but the hand of the diligent makes rich. He who gathers in the summer is a prudent son, but he who sleeps in harvest is a son who brings shame,"* [Proverbs 10:4-5].

David the King reminds us that, *"A good man sheweth favor and lendeth; he will guide his affairs with discretion,"* [Psalms 112:5].

Our efforts yield plenty that we are not hungry and have to share with others, *"He that tilleth his land shall have plenty of bread: but he that followeth after vain person shall have poverty enough,"* [Proverbs 28:19].

There are three scenarios spoken of here to keep in mind as it is certain that the Proverbial Woman did: He who is without the possibility of a stable income lives from day to day never knowing when poverty will attack them; A traveler, ever on the move, has not the stability of steady income; and a man with land, property too lazy to work paints a different picture; his poverty comes upon him because of laziness, sleeping refusing to take advantage of the blessings God has given him.

The Proverbial Woman is not of this sort, she diligently works, never allowing sleep to bring her and her family to poverty, nor allow her husband's wealth to dwindle away. She is ever vigilant, *"A little sleep, a little slumber, a little folding of the hands to rest, and poverty will come upon you like a robber, and want like an armed man,"* [Proverbs 6:10-11].

Paul tells us busy hands and busy minds are pleasing to God, *"I will therefore that the younger women marry, bear children, guide the house, give none occasion to the adversary to speak reproachfully,"* [I Timothy 5:14].

She does not have the time to be idle, it can and will cause error, and cause one io become displeasing to God. Paul encourages the older women to tutor the younger women, *"To be discreet, chaste, keepers at home, good, obedient to their own husbands, that the word of God be not blasphemed,"* [Titus 2:5].

The Proverbial Woman looked well to the ways of her household did not include just the physical care but also the spiritual. We cannot put all our time in gathering material things because they perish with the using; but we labor for the meat that is eternal; as well we, like the Proverbial Woman, look well to the ways of our household in all things. Ways are plural, "*Labour not for the meat which perisheth, but for that meat which endureth unto everlasting life, which the Son of man shall give unto you: for Him hath God the Father sealed,*" [*John 6:27*].

God knows all that we do whether evil or good, "*The eyes of the Lord are in every place, beholding the evil and the good,*" [*Proverbs 15:3*].

When one can exercise their authority with kindness; it is a gift of the Holy Spirit: they will rule with direction, have vision, and are found to be hateful or unreasonable because they have that power or authority. "*A Fruit of the Spirit,*" [*Ibid*].

Looking well to the ways of her household also includes her giving directions in a kind and godly manner, "*Or he that exhorteth, on exhortation: he that giveth, let him do it with simplicity; he that ruleth, with diligence; he that sheweth mercy, with cheerfulness,*" [*Romans 12:8*].

Looking well to the ways of her household also demands that she practice self-control (strength of mind) when she dealt with her household, the merchants, and neighbors.

Her example of kindness was needed in an overall arching way.

The Proverbial Woman was neither slothful nor negligent in her duties to her family, to her God, or to her neighbors. She did not suffer poverty of the Spirit to be pleasing to God nor poverty of material want for the things necessary to sustain life and limb.

V28: Her children rise up, and call her blessed; her husband also, and he praiseth her."

The name and reputation we have in life is defined by our character in life. Live a life so that even your name is remembered as being a righteous servant of God, even unto death and beyond. Listen at what Solomon said, *"A good man obtaineth favor from the Lord; but a man of wicked devices will He condemn,"* [Proverbs 12:2].

It is wise to obtain favor from the Lord rather than conduct oneself as is pleasing in their eyes; the end result of this choice, *"Therefore they shall eat the fruit of their own way and be filled to the full with their own fancies,"* [Proverbs 1:31].

"Yet a little sleep, a little slumber, a little folding of the hands to sleep: So, shall thy poverty come as one that travelleth, and thy want as an armed man," [Proverbs 6:10-11].

David paints a picture of the faithful and righteous in the sight of God, *"And he shall be like a tree planted by the rivers of water, that bringeth forth his fruit in his season; his leaf also shall not wither; and whatsoever he doeth shall prosper,"* [Psalms 1:3].

As well, *"A good man sheweth favour, and lendeth: he will guide his affairs with discretion. Surely, he shall not be moved forever: the righteous shall be in everlasting remembrance,"* [Psalms 112:5-6].

Moses reminds the people to keep their focus in the right place their blessing is from God and not of themselves, *"But thou say in thine heart, my power, and the might of mine hand hath gotten me this wealth. But thou shalt remember the Lord they God, for it is He that giveth thee power to get wealth, that thy mayeth establish His covenant which He swore unto thy father, as it is this day,"* [Deuteronomy 8:17-19].

God is impartial; He will bless the righteous on earth and punish the wicked. He does not choose the lesser for the more on earth. He will punish as well as bless because He is a righteous God without respect to person, *"Behold the righteous shall be recompensed in the earth; much more the wicked and the sinner,"* [Proverbs 11:31].

V29: Many daughters have done virtuously; but thou excellest them all."

The Proverbial Woman was busy each day with her duties, which is pleasing to God, *"Whosoever thy hands findeth to do, do with thy might; for there is no more work, nor device, nor knowledge, nor wisdom, in the grave whether thy goeth,"* [Ecclesiastes 9:10].

Moses reminds us that we are to, *"Therefore keep the words of this covenant and do them, they you may prosper in all that you do,"* [Deuteronomy 29:9].

We are to seek the Will of God and His Righteousness, we will then excel in the things that we do, *"Seek ye first the Kingdom of God and Its righteousness, and all these things will be added unto you,"* [Matthew 6:33].

The Preacher reminds us to, *"Sow your seed in the morning, and at evening let your hands not be idle, for you do not know which will succeed, whether this or that, or whether both will do equally well,"* [Ecclesiastes 6:11].

Paul cautions us we are to use each day to its fullest in our worship and serving God; it is profitable for us to, *"Redeem the times for the days are evil,"* [Ephesians 5:16].

Paul warns us further that, it shows wisdom when worshipping truly from the heart and not out of necessity, *"Which things have indeed a shew of wisdom in will worship, and humility, and neglecting of the body: not in any honour to the satisfying of the flesh,"* [Colossians 2:23].

Whatever we are doing it should be to the Glory of God, *"Not slothful in business; fervent in spirit; serving the Lord,"* [Romans 12:11].

"The way of the slothful man is as a hedge of thorns: but the way of the righteous is made plain," [Proverbs 15:19].

Being purposeful in our daily service to God shows wisdom; but not in an aimless manner; regardless of what it is, do it with all your might, with your focus on pleasing God, *"Therefore I do not run like someone running aimlessly; I do not fight like a boxer beating the air,"* [I Corinthians 9:26].

Business and riches can take wings and fly away if we are not careful to give honor to God rather than ourselves. We cannot allow our riches or success to blind us to who blessed us with those riches, *"For in one hour, so great riches, is come to naught and every shipmaster, and all the company in ships, and sailors, and as many as trade by sea, stood far off,"* [Revelations 18:17].

But *"Seek ye first the Kingdom of Heaven and its righteousness and these things will be added unto thee,"* [Matthew 6:33].

The Proverbial Woman does not live according to the world and the needs of her physical body and how the world lives, but according to the Will of God and His Commandments realizing through wisdom, all good and prefect gifts are from God who does not change, but continue to provide, for His children.

She does not dabble in the pleasure of the world, but remains vigilant and on task to be pleasing to God, *"Touch not; taste not; handle not; which are to perish with the using; after the commandments and the doctrine of men? Which things have indeed a show of wisdom in will worship, and humility and neglecting of the body; not in any honour to the satisfying of the flesh,"* [Colossians 2:21-23].

Time is a crucial factor in our lives as it was in the life of the Proverbial Woman. She does not waste time. We as Christians are to remain vigilant and careful in the use of our time utilizing it to the Glory of God and for the edification of self and others within our influence.

Paul the Apostle, tells us, that, we are to be mindful of, *"Redeeming the time because the days are evil,"* [Ephesians 5:16].

There was not a hint of laziness in the description of the Proverbial Woman and her day-to-day work, nor was there any with her maidens and servants, she set the example; she is the leader.

Paul in his letter to the Romans Christians, told them how they were to conduct themselves as people of God, wrote, *"Fervent in spirit, serving the Lord,"* [Romans 12:11b].

We can excel in the sight of God as the Proverbial Woman did; she is disciplined and works for the benefit of pleasing her Lord God and her husband. We can equate this to us today and women in the future generations with our focus on working to please our God and excel as she did so that we might hear

"Well done my good and faithful servant, come take your rest," [Ibid].

Paul wrote to the brethren at Corinth make your work and service beneficial to the Kingdom of God, *"I therefore run, not as uncertainty, so I fight, not as one that beateth the air," [I Corinthians 9:26].*

We are wise when focused, our services are meaningful, and we work to the honor and glory of God while on earth.

The Proverbial Woman walks in virtue and was pleasing to God; so, it is necessary with our walk to be pleasing to God.

The Proverbial Woman was not *"out of the way"* in her duty as a wife, home minister, and servant, but worked and served in a way that is pleasing to God.

We, like the Proverbial Woman, must be (*in the Way; not out of the Way*) in our duties and obedience to God.

The Scripture tells us of being *"in the Way"* when we obey the Gospel of Jesus Christ. Paul spoke of the *"Way"* in his defense before Felix that was considered a sect, which they told him was heresy. But we are in the *"Way"* as Proverbial Woman was, as Paul was, and all those who were before and will come after, when we are true worshippers and serve God as is commanded, *"But this I confess to you, that according to the Way, which they call a sect, I worship the God of our fathers, believing everything laid down by the Law and written in the Prophets," [Acts 24:14].*

Jesus said, He is the way, the truth, and the life, *"I am the Way, the Truth, and the Life: no man cometh unto the Father, but by Me," [John 14:6].*

We cannot continue to hear, and never understand; nor see, and never perceive.

The Proverbial Woman heard and understood; she saw and perceived the mighty ways of God and obeyed.

When I read about the attributes of the Proverbial Woman; she practiced the Beatitudes. The commands of Christ are a Christian's rule of duty as it was the law of the Servants of God, and the Proverbial Woman kept that rule of duty. We are to happiness, peace, and joy through Christ in this world and the next by that same rule of duty.

In the Beatitudes, Matthew 5th Chapter, we see the sixth commandment, the seventh commandment, and the Law of Love expressed:

V17-20: *6th Commandment,*

[Exodus 20:13], "Thou shall not Kill."

V12-27: *7th Commandment,*

[Exodus 20:14], "Thou shall not commit Adultery."

V38-42: *The Law of Love,*

[Romans 14:14-23], "I know and am convinced by the Lord Jesus that there is nothing unclean of itself; but to him who considers anything to be unclean, to him it is unclean. Yet if your brother is grieved because of your food, you are no longer walking in love. Do not destroy with your food the one for whom Christ died. Therefore, do not let your good be spoken of as evil; for the Kingdom of God is not eating and drinking, but righteousness and peace and joy in the Holy Spirit. For he who serves Christ in these things is acceptable to God and approved by men."

"Therefore, let us pursue the things which make for peace and the things by which one may edify another. Do not destroy the work of God for the sake of food. All things indeed are pure, but it is evil for the man who eats with offense. It is good neither to eat meat, drink wine, nor do anything by which your brother stumbles or is offended or is made weak. Do you have faith? Have it to yourself before God. Happy is he who does not condemn himself in what he approves. But he who doubts is condemned if he eats, because he does not eat from faith; for whatever is not from faith is sin."

We find that the Proverbial Woman practiced these Beatitudes and the Law of Love and was found pleasing to God, *"Owe no man anything, but to love one another: for he, that loveth another hath fulfilled the law," [Romans 13:8].*

Meekness brings blessings, *"Blessed are the meek: for they shall inherit the earth," [Matthew 5:5].*

Seeking God and the things of His Kingdom; we are to thirst for the Spiritual food and water, *"Blessed are they which do hunger and thirst after righteousness: for they shall be filled," [Matthew 5:6].*

Having a forgiving and tender heart toward all. We want our Heavenly Father to be merciful to us; we must in kind do the same, "*Blessed are the merciful: for they shall obtain mercy,*" *[Matthew 5:7].*

Servants are to have a pure heart before God, "*Blessed are the pure in heart: for they shall see God,*" *[Matthew 5:8].*

Wanting peace and being peaceful, "*Blessed are the peacemakers: for they shall be called the children of God,*" *[Matthew 5:9].*

The Christian Walk will bring challenges because we know we have an adversary, knowing that persecution will come we remain faithful to God we are blessed, "*Blessed are they which are persecuted for righteousness' sake: for theirs is the kingdom of heaven,*" *[Matthew 5:9].*

The faithful live their lives according to the virtues that our Savior demands, "*Ye are the salt of the earth: but if the salt have lost his savour, wherewith shall it be salted? it is thenceforth good for nothing, but to be cast out, and to be trodden under foot of men,*" *[Matthew 5:13].*

Live with honesty, truthfulness, and righteousness not as a hypocrite; say one thing and do another, "*Ye are the light of the world. A city that is set on a hill cannot be hid,*" *[Matthew 5:14].*

Never be ashamed of Christ by hiding your belief, "*Neither do men light a candle, and put it under a bushel, but on a candlestick; and it giveth light unto all that are in the house,*" *[Matthew 5:15].*

People of God are commanded to be full of good works which glorify God, "*Let your light so shine before men, that they may see your good works, and glorify your Father which is in heaven,*" *[Matthew 5:16].*

Christians cannot look and act righteous, but their hearts are not true to God, "*For I say unto you, that except your righteousness shall exceed the righteousness of the scribes and Pharisees, ye shall by no wise enter into the Kingdom of Heaven,*" *[Matthew 5:20].*

Do not speak in anger (Raca) to or another or speak to ruin their reputation; God considers it murder, "*Ye have heard that it was said of them of old time, thou shalt not kill; and whosoever shall kill shall be in danger of the judgment,*" *[Matthew 5:21].*

"To speak evil of no one, to avoid quarreling, to be gentle, and to show perfect courtesy toward all people," [Titus 3:2].

" So put away all malice, all deceit, hypocrisy, envy, and all slander," [I Peter 2:1].

Self-control is necessary in all areas of life, *"But I say unto you, that whosoever is angry with his brother without a cause shall be in danger of the judgment: and whosoever shall say to his brother, Raca, shall be in danger of the council: but whosoever shall say, thou fool, shall be in danger of hell fire," [Matthew 5:22].*

Control of your tongue, *"But let your communication be, yea, yea; nay, nay: for whatsoever is more than these cometh of evil," [Matthew 5:37].*

Selfishness is against the commandments of God, *"Give to him that asketh thee, and from him that would borrow of thee turn not thou away," [Matthew 5:42].*

God commands we love everyone regardless of who they are, Christ does; He gave His life for all, *"But I say unto you, love your enemies, bless them that curse you, do good to them that hate you, and pray for them which despitefully use you, and persecute you," [Matthew 5:44].*

God's providence is over all without exception, and we must have the same heart, *"That ye may be the children of your Father which is in heaven: for He maketh His sun to rise on the evil and on the good, and sendeth rain on the just and on the unjust," [Matthew 5:45].*

Scripture admonishes that people of God be perfect in heart and in mind willing to be humble and obedient before God and do as He command even when it is difficult, *"Be ye therefore perfect, even as your Father which is in heaven is perfect," [Matthew 5:48].*

Christians do not lay-up treasures on this earth but in heaven where they are eternal where there is no corruption of our works nor thieves can steal, *"Lay not up for yourselves treasures upon earth, where moth and rust doth corrupt, and where thieves break through and steal: but lay up for yourselves treasures in heaven, where neither moth nor rust doth corrupt, and where thieves do not break through nor steal," [Matthew 6:19-20].*

By hearing and obeying the Word of God is like building your house on a Rock (things of God) and he who hears and does not obey is compared to one building their house on sand (things of the world) which is moveable and unstable.

The Proverbial Woman built her house on the Rock where she could weather the storms of life and not on sand that has no stability, but washes away with the tides of time, *"Therefore whosoever heareth these sayings of mine, and doeth them, I will liken him unto a wise man, which built his house upon a rock: and the rain descended, and the floods came, and the winds blew, and beat upon that house; and it fell not: for it was founded upon a rock. And everyone that heareth these sayings of mine, and doeth them not, shall be likened unto a foolish man, which built his house upon the sand: And the rain descended, and the floods came, and the winds blew, and beat upon that house; and it fell: and great was the fall of it,"* [Matthew 7:24-27].

The principle that we serve God is based on what we do and why; that service must be done out of a pure heart when serving God not from an outward show to impress men.

The Proverbial Woman's life, as a Christian woman's life should be today, a life that lifts up our Savior before all and one that will be pleasing to God. Paul said in his letter to the Corinthians, *"Ye are our epistle, written in our hearts, known and read of all men,"* [2 Corinthians 3:2].

The Proverbial Woman was not rebellious, nor did she evade the duties of which God commands. She was not found disobedient to the Will of God for her life. We, as the Proverbial Woman, are in service to the God of Heaven, who changes not.

We see all these attributes in the description of the Proverbial Woman, *"Many have done virtuously, but thou excelleth them all,"* [Ibid].

The Proverbial Woman, we can ascertain from the Proverbs thirty-one tutorial, knew then what Paul the Apostle reminds us to do in this dispensation of time, *"Therefore, my beloved brethren, be ye steadfast, unmovable, always abounding in the work of the Lord, forasmuch as ye know that your labour is not in vain in the Lord,"* [I Corinthians 15:58].

V30: Favor is deceitful, and beauty is vain; but a woman that feareth the Lord, she shall be praised."

Beauty does not denote wisdom; it is an outward physical attribute and fades overtimes. God desires that we have the beauty that is inward (heart, soul, and spirit).

Beauty if fraudulent; it will lead you to believe it will last, but it does not. The beauty that last is the beauty of the heart, soul, and spirit, which will endure throughout eternity.

Our faithful service is beautiful to God, as we read of the beauty, of the heart, soul, and spirit as described of the Proverbial Woman.

The Proverbial Woman's influence is ubiquitous. Webster defines it as being found everywhere or permeating. Her influence was in abundance, it was found everywhere.

"A gracious woman retaineth honour: and strong men retain riches," [Proverbs 11:16].

Beauty without discretion is looked upon as being shameful, "Like a gold ring in a pig's snout is a beautiful woman without discretion," [Proverbs 11:22].

A gold ring in a pig's snout is useless, it is out of place, it does not fit the personality of a pig. The gold ring in his nose does not make him more desirable; nor does gold, silver, diamonds, or pearls on a beautiful woman lacking in discretion, makes her any more desirable; without a sense of decorum.

"The wisest of women builds her house, but folly with her hands tears it down," [Proverbs 14:1].

Being loud and acting without acumen is not to be name among the women of God, "A foolish woman is clamorous: she is simple, and knoweth nothing," [Proverbs 9:13].

The Proverbial Woman's beauty, which cannot be expressed enough, was both inward and outward; she had the heart and will to be a humble servant before God, "If thou knoweth not, O thou fairest among women go thy way forth by the footsteps of the flock, and feed thy kids besides the shepherd tent," [Solomon 1:8].

A gracious woman's honor will bring her a far better reward than the riches of the strong. A gracious woman's honor is lasting, riches take wings and fly away. It is better to have honor and beauty of the heart than riches, *"A gracious woman retaineth honor strong men retain riches," [Ibid].*

Her desire was to be godly and pleasing to God; and she strived for this goal. We can do the same thing or achieve the same goal. We all know what stresses and challenges comes each day that try our patience, try our ability to maintain self-control, yet we can; each challenge we overcome is another goal achieved as she did. Love was the fact that motivated her in all she does, the beauty of a godly woman.

The Proverbial woman, as house minister, had on a frequent basis, stressful days in her life with all she managed, yet she was patient, kind, and understanding.

Paul wrote, *"We are to live in such a way that no one will stumble because of us, and one will find fault with our ministry," [2 Corinthians 6:3].*

As well, *"But in all things approving ourselves as the ministers of God, in much patience, in afflictions, in necessities, in distresses," [2 Corinthians 6:4].*

Further, *"We are His workmanship created in Christ Jesus for good works, which God prepared beforehand so that we would walk in them," [Ephesians 2:10].*

Peter writes, *"Wherefore gird up the loins of your mind, be sober, and hope to the end for the grace that is to be brought unto you at the revelation of Jesus Christ. As obedient children, not fashioning yourselves according to the former lusts in your ignorance: But as He which hath called you is Holy, so be ye holy in all manner of conversation," I Peter 1:13-15].*

[Conversations come in more than just words; also, it is in our actions, decisions, and the way that we carry ourselves, choices we make, and the company we keep].

Our prayer to God must always be with a mournful heart before His throne that we might be pleasing to Him as we see expressed of the Proverbial Woman. David, in his Psalms, reminds us of the penitential spirit that the people of God need to be pleasing to Him, *"Create in me a clean heart, O God; and renew a right spirit within me," [Psalms 51:10].*

This beauty approved of by God is the Spirit of humility and obedience, not the physical beauty or beauty defined by the world.

V31: "Give her the fruit of her hands, and let her own work praise her in the gates."

The fear of the Lord builds wisdom each day, each year, with each experience adds to that wisdom – we began with fearing the Lord and through that fear comes wisdom; it is a gift of God, "*Every good and every perfect gift comes down from the Father of Lights of whom there is no variableness neither shadow of turning; of His own He begat us with the Word of Truth; that we should be a kind of first fruits of His creatures," [James 1:17-18].*

First fruits are the best God produces; Christ was the first fruit from the dead. The Proverbial Woman gave God her best in all things.

Righteousness is life to us as it was the Proverbial Woman, "*The fruit of the righteous is a tree of life; and he that winneth souls is wise," [Proverbs 11:30].*

Hard work and faithfulness are satisfying because she (we) labor as she (we) should and work so that we may have to give our families and have to share with others who are less fortunate so that it may be well with (her) us and as well as those she (we) can help provide for, "*For thou shalt eat the labour of thine hands: happy shalt thou be, and it shall be well with thee," [Psalms 128:2].*

The Proverbial Woman's works are a witness to her heart and faithfulness toward God as ours could (should) be, "*We shall know them by their fruits. Do men gather grapes of thorns, or figs of thistles? Wherefore by their fruits ye shall know them," [Matthew 7:16,20].*

The Proverbial Woman's fruit of holiness bought her everlasting life and peace. The fruit that we bear (works) will in the end bring us everlasting life and peace, "*What fruit did you have then in the things of which you are now ashamed? For the end of those things is death. But now having been set free from sin, and having become slaves of God, you have your fruit to holiness, and the end, everlasting life," [Romans 6:21-22].*

Paul reminds us that all that we do in the Name of the Lord is credited to our account of faithfulness before God; it was not for himself he wanted anything from the Christians at Philippi. He encourages them to give for their benefits and blessings bearing fruit toward God, "*Not because I desire a gift: but I desire fruit that may abound to your account," [Philippians 4:17].*

We, as the Proverbial Woman, should have examples of the good works of a faithful servant and kindness to her (our) neighbors and those who are less fortunate. The Scripture gives Dorcas along with the Proverbial Woman as an excellent example of a woman of good works, *"Then Peter arose and went with them. When he was come, they brought him into the upper chamber: and all the widows stood by him weeping, and shewing the coats and garments which Dorcas made, while she was with them," [Acts 9:39].*

Paul commended Women in Scripture for their faithfulness, good works, and the fruit they bore, *"I commend unto you Phebe our sister, which is a servant of the church which is at Cenchrea: That ye receive her in the Lord, as becometh saints, and that ye assist her in whatsoever business she hath need of you: for she hath been a succourer of many, and of myself also. Greet Priscilla and Aquila my helpers in Christ Jesus: Who have for my life laid down their own necks: unto whom not only I give thanks, but also all the churches of the Gentiles. Greet Mary, who bestowed much labour on us. Salute Tryphena and Tryphosa, who labour in the Lord. Salute the beloved Persis, which laboured much in the Lord," [Romans 16:1-4;6,12].*

Paul, the Apostle reminds us that our good works will be evident to all, *"Likewise, also the good works of some are manifest beforehand; and they that are otherwise cannot be hid," [I Timothy 5:25].*

God is faithful in His promises to us; man forgets, God does not, *"For God is not unrighteous to forget your work and labour of love, which ye have shewed toward His name, in that ye have ministered to the saints, and do minister," [Hebrews 6:10].*

We are blessed when we are faithful to God and do His Will, *"And I heard a voice from heaven saying unto me, Write, Blessed are the dead which die in the Lord from henceforth: Yea, saith the Spirit, that they may rest from their labours; and their works do follow them," [Revelations 14:13].*

The Proverbial Woman's beauty and good works as should ours be, are of the heart, *"Favour is deceitful, and beauty is vain: but a woman that feareth the Lord, she shall be praised," [Proverbs 31:30].*

Man, in and of himself, cannot gain wisdom, not the wisdom that pleases God and enables one to serve the Heavenly Father in the manner that is pleasing to Him. He does not refuse His people wisdom: we, but need to ask, *"If any lack wisdom, let him ask of God, that giveth to all men liberally, and upbraideth not; and it shall be given him," [James 1:1-5].*

The Proverbial Woman knew, believed, and depended upon God, as we should know, believe, and depend upon God, *"My flesh and my heart faileth: but God is the strength of my heart, and my portion forever,"* [Psalms 73:26].

Paul reminds us that serving God as Scripture commands is wisdom though it be inconvenient, seems strange, or outdated God knows what is best for His children, *"And we know all things work together for the good to them that love God and to them who are called according to [His] purpose,"* [Romans 8:28].

"Moreover, whom [He] did predestinate, them [He] also called: and whom [He] called, them [He] also justified: and whom [He] justified, them [He] also glorified," [Romans 8:30].

The Proverbial Woman knew, as we know, that it is only gain in serving God and being faithful to His word. We do not lose, though it seems at times we do, yet God sustains us and if faithful to the end our names will be written in the Book of Life. Paul wrote concerning the faithful women who worked in the Kingdom of God and their names are in the Book of Life, *"Yes, and I ask you, loyal yokefellow, help these women who have contended at my side in the cause of the gospel, along with Clement and the rest of my fellow workers, whose names are in the book of life,"* [Philippians 4:3].

The Proverbial Woman praises are seen throughout the thirty-first chapter of the Book of Proverbs and is summed up in this manner, because she is found to be pleasing to God. She is given credit for her works because they were notable and she was praised because she excelled; not because she was perfect, but because she was obedient, faithful, loving, caring, kind, honorable, hardworking, an excellent mother, good example, a faithful wife, a help meet for he husband and most important a servant of God, and *"Give her the fruit of her hands, and let her own work praise her in the gates,"* [Ibid].

She was a faithful wife and true helpmeet for her husband, which is pleasing to God, *"And the Lord God said, It is not good that the man should be alone; I will make him a help meet for him,"* [Genesis 2:18].

EPILOGUE

Proverbs thirty-one begins with the advice of a mother to her son and three questions she posed to the son of her womb, the son of her love and the son of her vows. The responsibilities of his kingdom and its people are enormous, and his focus must be on his rule. The way he rules must be above all, pleasing to God, allowing Him to direct his path, and praying for wisdom that all he does is according of the commands of the God of Heaven.

Important to his rule are the duties of righteous judgments, speaking for those who are less fortunate who has no voice (the poor), judge without respect of persons; essentially, being attentive to all detail. She warned him to be aware of the dangers of the people who are around him, the evils of strong drink, wine, partying, and adulterous and strange women.

A king's reputation must be above reproach and is found to be faithful in all his duties so that his kingdom will not fall. And above all, the choice of a godly woman who will be a "help meet" to him in all that he does. A wife who is a true home minister that his mind might be relieved knowing that she if faithfully executing those duties so that his focus can be on the people, his kingdom.

Each generation must thread that needle of obedience and continue to eliminate the things of the world that beset humans and bestir self in the direction that God commands. It is difficult to live a life that is pleasing to God in this day and time with all the attractions of the knowledge, choices, and modernism out there, but it can be done.

However, there is modernism in everyone's generation and as this generation passes, the next one will see our generation as antiquated as we see others. No matter the attractiveness of the things of the world, which is a challenge, we can overcome and learn from practice how to thread that needle and live based on those principles expressed in the Biblical account of the Proverbial Woman and we will be, like she was, pleasing of God.

The Proverbial Woman eliminated the noise of the world and focused on her duties and responsibilities as a servant of God, a wife, a mother, a businesswoman, a decision maker, a merchant, an employer, an example to her maiden, and the overall community.

She did not just do these things physically; she wore those Spiritual garments of faithfulness, righteousness, dedication, and did not allow the world to influence her decision or actions, when it comes to right/wrong, good/evil.

There are three idols in this world that Satan continually put before man: the lust of the flesh, the lust of the eye, and the pride of life.

She eliminated these and cleave unto God and His commandments for her life.

The Proverbial Woman did not allow herself to fall into a state of unawareness to the trouble of others. As well, we have the same command from God to share with and help those who are less fortunate. Doing well in life does not excuse God's people from the dictum of helping those who are less fortunate, *"Distributing to the necessity of saints; given to hospitality," [Romans 12:13].*

The Scripture describes the Proverbial Woman as being exemplary in this as well; she assisted the poor along with caring for her household. She shared her blessings from God with others in a pleasing manner to the Heavenly Father.

She did not offend God for the lack of a giving spirit with her material or Spiritual blessings.

Let us be about service to God in doing His work on earth, not relaxing, or lounging in ease in our blessings or worldly possessions and be mindful of the message that Amos the Prophet delivered from God to His people, *"Woe to them that are at ease in Zion, and trust in the mountain of Samaria, which are named chief of the nations, to whom the house of Israel came! Pass ye unto Calneh, and see; and from thence go ye to Hamath the great: then go down to Gath of the Philistines: be they better than these kingdoms? or their border greater than your border? That lie upon beds of ivory, and stretch themselves upon their couches, and eat the lambs out of the flock, and the calves out of the midst of the stall; ye that put far away the evil day, and cause the seat of violence to come near; that chant to the sound of the viol, and invent to themselves instruments of musick, like David; that drink wine in bowls, and anoint themselves with the chief ointments: but they are not grieved for the affliction of Joseph,"*

"Therefore, now shall they go captive with the first that go captive, and the banquet of them that stretched themselves shall be removed. The Lord God hath sworn by Himself, saith the Lord the God of Hosts, I abhor the excellency of Jacob, and hate his palaces: therefore will I deliver up the city with all that is therein," [Amos 6:1-8].

It is easy to get comfortable in our doing well materially and forget there are those who are less fortunate than we, who needs our assistance.

We have the tools to follow the Proverbial Woman's example to build that life through Jesus Christ Our Savior who provided Salvation and with the help of the Holy Spirit who is our teacher and guide.

Everything we do should be done in God's name, according to His will and be directed toward our glorifying His name and authority over our lives, "*And whatsoever ye do in word or deed, do all in the name of the Lord Jesus, giving thanks to God the Father by Him," [Colossians 3:17].*

Our way of living should be a sacrifice to Christ, as His life was sacrificed for us. Our devotion should be to Him not to what we want over His will and commands. We see all of this in the example of the Proverbial Woman and her devotion to God and her duties as a faithful wife.

We read in the New Testament, specifically in the Book of Acts, two examples of women doing what they can to help the poor and being enterprising and independent women.

Lydia was a seller of purple, she ordered from afar. Purple was expensive and considered to be the dress of a King, "*And a certain woman named Lydia, a seller of purple, of the city of Thyatira, which worshipped God, heard us: whose heart the Lord opened, that she attended unto the things which were spoken of by Paul," [Acts 16:14].*

Dorcas (Tabitha) did good, whatsoever her hands found to do. She made garments for her fellow sisters. She used her gifts from God and her resources to bless others, "*Now there was at Joppa a certain disciple named Tabitha, which by interpretation is called Dorcas: this woman was full of good works and alms deeds which she did. And it came to pass in those days, that she was sick, and died: whom when they had washed, they laid her in an upper chamber. And forasmuch as Lydda was nigh to Joppa, and the disciples had heard that Peter was there, they sent unto him two men, desiring him that he would not delay to come to them,"*

"*Then Peter arose and went with them. When he was come, they brought him into the upper chamber: and all the widows stood by him weeping, and shewing the coats and garments which Dorcas made, while she was with them. But Peter put them all forth, and kneeled down, and prayed; and turning him to the body said, Tabitha, arise. And she opened her eyes: and when she saw Peter, she sat up. And he gave her his hand, and lifted her up, and when he had called the saints and widows, presented her alive. And it was known throughout all Joppa; and many believed in the Lord," [Acts 9:36–42].*

When thinking of the Proverbial Woman the scores of descriptions of what she does, demonstrates the diversity of talents she has, the wisdom she uses in dealing with merchants, and the confidence she had in her ability to make the decision in what areas to make use of her wealth: yet, never forgetting the duties of a wife, mother, friend, and supervisor.

We can identify the different hats the Proverbial Woman wears as do women of this century and bygone eras as well. We can know that there were people whose life she touched who saw God in her life. Her day-to-day life and example showed those around her the nature of the God she served.

In today's world, women continue to wear a multiplicity of hats. The Proverbial Woman paints a portrait for women. There is room on the canvas for each of us. Where each woman may not have the abundance of skills sets or do not do all these things done by her, these are all tasks, at intervals, in our lives, we as women all do, have done, or will do in our duties as wives, mothers, neighbors, servants, and friends.

Each of these tasks are not something she does every day, but she does one or more of these daily sometimes different than she did yesterday. We do things on an as need basis sometimes, but these duties are always in our "things to do" bag.

We should not show ingratitude for God's blessing and mercy; serving Christ and His commands are the same as serving God, for they are one. We give God our best, the first fruit of our increase, not what is left or our service after we have put ourselves first, *"I and My Father are one. A son honoureth His father, and a servant his master: if then I be a Father, where is My honour? and if I be a Master, where is my fear? saith the Lord of Hosts unto you, O priests, who despise My name. And ye say, Wherein have we despised Thy name? Ye offer polluted bread upon Mine altar; and ye say, Wherein have we polluted Thee? In that ye say, The table of the Lord is contemptible. And if ye offer the blind for sacrifice, is it not evil? And if ye offer the lame and sick, is it not evil? Offer it now unto thy governor; will he be pleased with thee, or accept thy person? saith the Lord of Hosts?"*

"From the rising of the sun even unto the going down of the same, My Name shall be great among the Gentiles; and in every place incense shall be offered unto My Name, and a pure offering: for My Name shall be great among the heathen, saith the Lord of

Hosts. But ye have profaned It, in that ye say, the table of the Lord is polluted; and the fruit thereof, even His meat, is contemptible. Ye said also, Behold, what a weariness is it! and ye have snuffed at It, saith the Lord of Hosts; and ye brought that which was torn, and the lame, and the sick; thus, ye brought an offering: should I accept this of your hand? saith the Lord. But cursed be the deceiver, which hath in his flock a male, and voweth, and sacrificeth unto the Lord a corrupt thing: for I am a great King, saith the Lord of Hosts,' [Malachi 1,12,13,14].

We love Him because He first loved us. Our relationship is compared to the Priests who defied His commands, if we want a relationship with God, it obliges us to fear and give honor and praise for He is the Great and Holy God without stain or blemish, righteous in His judgment, and just in His punishment.

We do no want God to question our faithfulness, our giving Him bad fruit, or will worship, unclean sacrifices, or lip service. God desires and deserves the best, the fruit of our faithfulness, presenting our bodies as living sacrifices holy and acceptable in His service, and speaking truth in kindness and righteousness in all things pertaining to life and godliness.

Our worship and service to God must not be contemptible or show contempt. Malachi compared human slothfulness in worship as bringing before God the lame, sick, blind, and it is an evil. We do not offer people of authority here on earth such contemptible things, we do our best in our service or jobs so then so much more should we offer our best to Christ our Savior, God our Father, and the Holy Spirit our Teacher and Guide, *"And if ye offer the blind for sacrifice, is it not evil? and if ye offer the lame and sick, is it not evil? offer it now unto thy governor; will he be pleased with thee, or accept thy person? saith the Lord of Hosts,"* [Malachi 1:8].

God is merciful but will not indulge man in their blatant sins or disregard our not honoring, worshipping, and obeying Him as commanded. We are to give Him our best. He gave us His best, Jesus Christ Our Lord, and Savior.

We cannot profane the worship of God because we do not worship Him from the heart but from outward necessity. Humans falling into a state of indifference is an evil perpetrated by Satan. Slipping into a state of being lethargic has consequences both here in this world and in eternity.

Christians cannot allow themselves to fall into a state of apathy.

By continuing to fight each day the battle of Christianity, God can be served in the manner He commands and deserve as the God and Creator of all mankind. Indifference is a choice as Scripture reminds us, *"Choose ye this day whom you will serve," [Joshua 25:15].*

If we are not serving the God of Heaven, then we are under the control of Satan our adversary.

The Proverbial Woman were, as we are, employed by God in His service. We, as she, are Priest … and Priests who serve God in His Holy Temple. Our Temple is our bodies honoring our God with our lives and services offering sacrifices of heart, mind, lips, body, soul, and spirit in faithfulness.

We are Spiritual Priests as Paul the Apostle reminds us. We must lead people in the right direction according to God's commands in the way that we live and teach; being knowledgeable of the Scripture.

Wisdom is needed as God gives liberally to all who desire and pray for it, *"If any of you lack wisdom, let him ask of God, that giveth to all men liberally, and upbraideth not; and it shall be given him," [James 1:5].*

Wisdom is a gift from Heaven, *"All good and perfect gifts come down from the Father of Lights whom there is no variableness or shadow of turning," [James 1:17].*

Our lives should give glory to His name, Malachi gave the people the warning from God, *"If ye will not hear, and if ye will not lay it to heart, to give glory unto My name, saith the Lord of Hosts, I will even send a curse upon you, and I will curse your blessings: yea, I have cursed them already, because ye do not lay it to heart," [Malachi 2:2].*

The Proverbial Woman was viewed by God and her husband in an overall positive manner. She was her husband's closes relationship, even more so than his mother and father and she had a close and reverent relationship with God.

A man leaves his father and mother and cleave unto his wife, and they shall become one flesh, *"Therefore shall a man leave his father and his mother and shall cleave unto his wife: and they shall be one flesh," [Genesis 2:24].*

God created woman out of man, *"Then the Lord God made a woman from the rib He had taken out of the man, and He brought her to the man. The man said, "This is now bone of my bones and flesh of my flesh; she shall be called 'woman,' for she was taken out of man," [Genesis 2:22-24].*

117

Our hearts are the temple of God, prepared by God through His Holy Scriptures, to be harbingers of His message of Salvation to others. We are to spread or share the Gospel with others. We see the Proverbial Woman living the righteous life through her actions and wisdom of her words. In doing so she was spreading the goodness and faithfulness of God toward His people.

Jesus is like a refiner fire and like fuller soap which has cleansing factors to them eliminating the dross of our lives, *"But who can endure the day of His coming? Who can stand when He appears? For He will be like a refiner's fire or a launderer's soap. He will sit as a refiner and purifier of silver; He will purify the Levites and refine them like gold and silver. Then the Lord will have men who will bring offerings in righteousness,"* [Malachi 3:2-3].

We as women of God are Pearls in the Kingdom. A pearl is refined overtime in the Oyster and when fully formed has a beautiful luster to them, *"On the day when I act,"* says the Lord Almighty, *"they will be My treasured possession. I will spare them, just as a father has compassion and spares his son who serves him,"* [Malachi 3:17].

He loves us because we are obedient servants not because we are perfect, but willing to submit to His will for our lives. It is wisdom to live in humility and obedience before God.

The *[thirty-nineth chapter of Job]* spoke of man's weakness before the Almighty God. Chapter *[thirty-nine]* expresses the limits of man and his weakness before the God of Heaven creator of all things using the examples of powerful animals to express man's inability to stand against His Power, how sinful man is, and its fatal consequences.

It is folly and lack of wisdom blinded by sin to think we can escape the wrath of God, for our disobedience.

Love for our Savior helps us to remember Christ stripped off His Robe of Righteousness and became flesh that our sins be covered by His Blood. He provided Salvation through His willingness to take upon Himself the sins of the world and hang on that cruel cross of Calvary.

Wisdom demands that we be clothed in righteous through the Word of God, *"The steps of a good man are ordered by the Lord and he delighteth in His way,"* [Psalms 37:23].

And *"The mouth of the righteous speaketh wisdom, and his tongue talketh of judgment,"* *[Psalms 37:30]*.

Sin is like a cloud; it separates man from the light of God. We cannot see God living in darkness; He is hidden by the face of sin and disobedience which blocks the light of Salvation, as the clouds does the sun.

Sin's character causes the prolonging of misery to worsen overtime. The longer man indulges therein the further we get from God.

In the Book of Job, we can consider these questions God asked him:

➢ **Can a man darken the Council of God?" [Job 38:2].**
➢ **Is this not provoking our Heavenly Father?**
➢ **Do we know more than God? [Job 38:2].**
➢ **Hast, thou commanded the morning since thy days; and caused the dayspring to know his place?" [Job 38:12].**

Paul reminds us that, *"Christ is the Day-Spring from on High,"* *[2 Corinthians 4:6]*.

The Proverbial Woman redeemed the time she had each day that she had another opportunity to live. She did not waste a minute of her time even at night her candle did not go out, *"Redeem the time, because the days are evil,"* *[Ibid]*.

We cannot roll time forward, borrow from tomorrow, or slip back and correct yesterday. Those things we can do, do them today, because no one knows if he or she will be alive or healthy or when or if a tomorrow will come for you.

The Proverbial Woman as often mentioned, was diligent. She did the work assigned to her as the wife, mother, friend, advisor, and guider of her household. The trust her husband had in her to use that time wisely and take care of the home ministry shines in the Biblical description of the Proverbial Woman – a woman with the characteristics and attributes that are pleasing to God.

No matter how long or short our time on earth is, we can use the years and days to their fullest not wasting the time with which we could be serving God.

Scripture asks and answers the question about our life and time here on earth through a thought-provoking question and declarative answer:

➢ *"What is your life? it is but a vapor!" [James 4:14b]*.

A vapor is a puff of steam, or smoke that appears but a moment in time and it dissipates just as quickly as it appears.

We are reminded in Scripture as well that, *"But, beloved, be not ignorant of this one thing, that one day is with the Lord is a thousand years, and a thousand years as one day,"* [2 Peter 3:8].

The years of man are three score and ten and if by reason of strength they are eighty years," [Psalms 90:10].

Seventy or eight years, even beyond is but a speck of time in a day in one's life in reference to one thousand years. That portion of a day is not exceptionally long then we fly away to an eternity of peace either with God or an eternity of suffering without God.

Serving God is man's main purpose on earth. God created us to serve Him. He gave His only begotten Son, Our Lord, and Savior Jesus Christ that we might be saved and create a path back to Him. He has created every avenue for man's Salvation. We can never repay or do enough to thank God for His mercy and grace.

However, we can do as He asks and serve Him in the way He commands, and He will be pleased. We each have a choice, *"Choose ye this day whom you will serve; if it be the gods on the other side of the river then serve them,"* but listen to the wisdom of Joshua in the second half of that Scripture, *"But for me and my house, we will serve God,"* [Joshua 24:15].

The Proverbial Woman in her God-given wisdom demonstrated through her dutiful dedication the profitability of both spiritually and physically serving God.

Our work for God is here on earth that we might inherit an eternity of peace with God the Father, God the Son, and God the Holy Spirit.

Paul reminds us we are given the Holy Spirit as a down payment on that inheritance.

The world that Satan presents as being "do as you please" is fluid and dangerous, not only now but for eternity. He is good at deception; we are to stay on task, attend our duties, take care of our responsibilities to our family, and lastly serve God with all thy might, and we would have not the time to be busy bodies in other men matters, gossip, or waste time; but should redeem that time for our Lord and the work He left for us to do on our sojourn here.

Isaiah cautioned not to be [*out of the way*]; [*Ibid*].

The entire chapter of [*Proverbs 31*] is a look into what we are to do in this life, and the fleeting moments of time in which we have do it.

The description of the Proverbial Woman is not in an ebb and flow manner – she is assiduous in her dedication and duties to her family which include (husband, children, maids, and workers).

When we do the things, we are to do, as God commands, then we are pleasing to Him. She did not neglect her responsibilities.

We have examples of the people's disobedience before God and what they suffered. This Scripture serves as a warning when we do not take care of our responsibilities or duties, we will not be pleasing to God; as well, when we take care of our responsibilities or duties and are pleasing to God, "*Thing written aforetime are written for our learning that we through the patience and comfort of the Scripture might have hope*," [*Romans 15:4-5*].

We were all young at one time, as all women will have been but, as we age and become spiritually wiser, have the responsibility of instructing the younger women; it is like paying it forward for the next Christian generation of women. We all help and assist others, "*Older women are to teach the young women to love their husbands and children. They are to teach them to think before they act, to be pure, to be workers at home, to be kind, and to obey their own husbands. In this way, the Word of God is honored. Also teach young men to be wise*," [*Titus 2:4-6*].

We as mothers, as did King Lemuel's mother, are to tutor the young men or our sons to be wise, "*Iron sharpeneth iron; so, a man sharpeneth the countenance of his friend*," [*Proverbs 27:17*].

As we associate and fellowship with others, we can have an influence on them by letting them see us using our wisdom to teach and train as we saw in the example of the Proverbial Woman with her maidens and other workers; by this we help and assist others so they can help and assist those around them. It is so important that we be conscious of the people we are around; it is so easy to adopt their unhealthy habits without realizing it; thereby becoming displeasing to God: And in contrast, we can adopt their healthy habits and be pleasing to God.

God blesses us daily with care; our needs He fulfills in food, clothing, and all the things necessary for life. He gave us the skills and knowledge to make a living. But above all those daily blessings, He purchased our Salvation.

Daily Christ is fulfilling His promises of being with us to the end; He sent His Holy Spirit as a guarantee and our teacher and guide during our sojourn, *"Blessed be the Lord, who daily loadeth us with benefits, even the God of our Salvation. Selah, "[Psalms 68:19].*

He is a shelter for us in our walk toward eternity, *"Thou art my hiding place; thou shall preserve me from trouble; thou shall compass me about with songs of deliverance. Selah," [Psalms 32:7].*

Christ is there to sustain us through trials and tribulations, *"Cast they burdens upon the Lord, and He shall sustain thee; He shall never suffer the righteous to be moved, "[Psalms 55:22].*

He is from everlasting to everlasting, *"His name shall be continued as long as the sun: and men shall be blessed in Him: all nations shall call Him blessed. Praise be to the Lord God, the God of Israel who alone does marvelous deeds," [Psalms 72:17-18].*

His promises are to never forsake or leaves us, *"And even to your old age I am He; and ever to hoar hairs I will carry you: I have made, and will bear, even I will carry, and will deliver you," [Isaiah 46:4].*

"Blessed be the God and Father of our Lord Jesus Christ, who has blessed us in Christ with every spiritual blessing in the heavenly places, even as He chose us in Him before the foundation of the world, that we should be holy and blameless before Him," [Ephesians 1:3-4].

God is compassionate each day that come. We can see it each day without fail; His compassion endureth. As things and portions on this earth perish as the Scripture tells us, Christ is our portion that never fails; but is eternal.

We are to wait on the Lord with hope and patience, *"The Lord is good unto them that wait for Him, to the soul that seeketh Him. It is good that man should both hope and quietly wait for the Salvation of the Lord. It is of the Lord's mercies that we are not consumed, because His compassions fail not. They are new every morning: great is thy faithfulness," [Lamentations 3:22-26].*

122

"For our God is our God forever and ever; He will be our guide even unto death," [Psalms 48:14].

God does not change His mind when He promises us something; He performs all promises without fail when we are faithful, *"For the gifts and callings of God are irrevocable,"* [Romans 11:29].

The training ground is here on earth. We cannot have the peaceful end without the beginning. Serving God is necessary while here on earth to inherit eternity. We cannot live the way we so choose and expect to have an eternity of peace.

The produce in our Spiritual Gardens grow from the seeds we planted.

We must work while here; Salvation was purchased for us. Our works cannot earn us Salvation; however, Salvation earned us the opportunity to do the work Christ left us to do while we are here that we might inherit eternity. Paul the Apostle tell us in this manner, *"Wherefore, my beloved, as ye have always obeyed, not as in my presence only, but now much more in my absence, work out your own salvation with fear and trembling,"* [Philippians 2:12-13].

The Proverbial Woman was profitable to the Kingdom of God – through her excellent work. Her daily walk was one of faithfulness, honesty, integrity, and ethics. She was a good example for all to see and read about through the descriptions given in Scripture.

Women of God can glean from the example of the Proverbial Woman and make application in their lives.

We must harness this wisdom that we might in and with as much effort as we can, take our binoculars of spiritual vision, and look back through time, and glean from the wisdom King Lemuel's Mother taught him and teach the next generation including our daughters and granddaughters; as well, and those who through our lives can be influenced by being that example of how we can be pleasing to God and what will be pleasing to God.

The *[Proverbs 31]* Tutorial is beneficial for life and pursuit of spiritual happiness in the Lord. Joy cannot be found or harnessed from the world.

> ➢ **The way we choose to live is ours; the choices are: pain and misery living like the world dictates or living as Scripture commands, which is joy and hope of eternal peace with God; which one will you chose?**
> ➢ **Stop and take an assessment of yourself, what did you see?**
> ➢ **What skills do you have that you can identify that God has blessed you with?**

Think of what the Apostle Peter counseled in reference to adding qualities to our lives overtime, *"And beside this, giving all diligence, add to your faith virtue; and to virtue knowledge; And to knowledge temperance; and to temperance patience; and to patience godliness; And to godliness brotherly kindness; and to brotherly kindness charity. For if these things be in you, and abound, they make you that ye shall neither be barren nor unfruitful in the knowledge of our Lord Jesus Christ. But he that lacketh these things are blind, and cannot see afar off, and hath forgotten that he was purged from his old sins,"* [2 Peter 1:5-9].

We cannot attain to all these attributes in one sitting; but note that the Apostle said, *"add to."*

These comes with our efforts and application of God's Word, based on the principles laid out by the descriptions in the *[Thirty-first Chapter of Proverbs]*.

King Lemuel's Mother said these are the attributes and the like that a King (man) should look for when he is seeking a wife, beginning with her being a godly woman; a woman of morals, ethics, integrity, humility, not prideful, but kind, hardworking, focusing on her family first, and work outward.

A wife could and should be a support system for her husband, the home minister that he can trust to do what is right in all things. Whose good name precedes her, and he can be well-spoken of and not suffer embarrassment because of her or her actions. Regardless of the amount of wealth one might have those riches cannot buy you a good name. Wealth comes and goes, but your reputation stays with you no matter where you go, *"A good name is rather to be chosen than great riches, and loving favour rather than silver and gold,"* [Proverbs 22:1].

A good name last longer than riches.

The Proverbial Woman from the reading of the text had both wealth and a good name. Many can have wealth, but a bad reputation, therefore their riches does not serve them in a positive manner.

The Proverbial Woman is based on a principle that, shows the contents of her heart and how she is to view her duties, her responsibilities, her faithfulness to her husband in all things, and most importantly, how she views the God she serves and what she must be willing to give up in the worldly realm that she might be viewed by the God of the Universe as excelling in all things.

It is evident that the Proverbial Woman did not overvalue worldly wealth but valued her relationship with God and her family as the wealth in her life; she worked in the realm of her duties and was pleasing to God, "*Thou excelleth them all,*" *[Ibid].*

Scripture reminds us that evil, envy, and covetousness are the result of the gods of this world that men make for themselves and serve rather than the God of Heaven.

The Proverbial Woman did not allow her worldly wealth to cause pride to overtake her and forget the one and only God she served and knew from whence comes her blessings.

She excels in righteousness and is an example of what we are commanded to do today, "*That they may teach the young women to be sober, to love their husbands, to love their children, to be discreet, chaste, keepers at home, good, obedient to their own husbands, that the word of God be not blasphemed,*" *[Titus 2:4-5].*

Older is not always defined by age but can be defined by a woman's maturity in her spiritualty teaching through her wisdom and experience as she serves God and is faithfully executing her duties and responsibilities. We can see the Proverbial Woman was mature and used her ability to prioritize.

> ➢ **What are your priorities in this life each day?**
> ➢ **Do you put God first in all things?**
> ➢ **Do your actions show how you view what God command for His people?**

We know that we do not all mature at the same rate in the gospel or in our service to God. So, those who are mature can or should set the example or extend a strong arm of wisdom for those who do not grow as fast, by being that example, having patience, showing kindness, lending understanding, and all done through knowledge as the first chapter of second Peter admonishes in reference to adding to those virtues.

Traveling the path of righteousness is not an easy journey; therefore, we can remind ourselves that we once traveled that path of immaturity in the Gospel, and so will our younger sisters until they mature.

Christ has patience, can we have any less with the immaturity of our sisters in Christ?

When looking at the text of the Proverbial Woman, let us have the right view and appreciation for this wisdom and not be found guilty of not employing that wisdom.

Paul reminds us that, *"Things written aforetime are written for our learning that we through patience and comfort of the Scripture might have hope," [Romans 15:4].*

The Proverbial Woman is a written treasure for our benefit; it is like finding a pearl, a valuable pearl like the man who finds the treasure in the field and went and purchased the field to have that treasure.

He did not just want the treasure, but the responsibilities of everything that comes with that treasure, *"Again, the Kingdom of Heaven is like unto treasure hid in a field, which when a man hath found, he hideth, and for joy thereof goeth and selleth all that he hath, and buyeth that field," [Matthew 13:44].*

He considered it of such value he desired to possess not just the treasure but the field; selling everything he had to possess it.

> ➤ **Is that same joy there for you in being in the Kingdom of Heaven? That is a question each Christian must ask themselves.**
> ➤ **Are you willing to give up your life in the world and come to Christ and serve Him as commanded?**

There is always more treasure in the Word of God to find. The Scripture is a Pearl of great Value that we can benefit from it Spiritually for an eternity if we grab hold and follow Jesus.

The description of the Proverbial Woman given here is an honor from God for a mother, wife, neighbor, friend, and servant in the Kingdom.

Let us not look at it as being in servitude and as a dishonor, but as a great honor. Naturally, we are doing all these things to the glory of God and being appreciated by our families and husband as a pearl of immense value when she is a faithful godly woman.

Herein we find that the Proverbial Woman was of great value and seen by her husband as a treasure in his life.

God is pleased with our dedication and faithfulness as mothers, wives, and servants in His Kingdom and the fact that we are willing to obey the standards that He sets in our lives.

We cannot live anyway we desire and think that God will be pleased.

It takes humility to submit our lives to God's will; bringing our entire self in subjection, which is heart, mind, body, soul, and spirit.

Ezekiel gave a vivid description of the power and beauty of God. The images that the Priest saw of the all-knowing, all-seeing, and all-powerful God; and the way the people of God should be faithful, persistent, strong, unwavering in direction and obedience to God as He is to His Children.

Reading the description should allow man to see the Creator and His all-seeing ability, nothing or no one can escape His judgment or prevent His blessings. He sets up and brings down whom He choses regardless of who we are cannot escape the Creator, *"The word of the Lord came expressly unto Ezekiel the Priest, the son of Buzi, in the land of the Chaldeans by the River Chebar; and the hand of the Lord was there upon him. And I looked, and behold, a whirlwind came out of the north, a great cloud, and a fire infolding itself, and a brightness was about it, and out of the midst thereof as the colour of amber, out of the midst of the fire. Also, out of the midst thereof came the likeness of four living creatures. And this was their appearance; they had the likeness of a man. And everyone had four faces, and everyone had four wings. And their feet were straight feet; and the sole of their feet was like the sole of a calf's foot: and they sparkled like the colour of burnished brass. And they had the hands of a man under their wings on their four sides; and they four had their faces and their wings. Their wings were joined one to another; they turned not when they went; they went everyone straight forward. As for the likeness of their faces, they four had the face of a man, and the face of a lion, on the right side: and they four had the face of an ox on the left side; they four also had the face of an eagle. Thus were their faces: and their wings were stretched upward; two wings of every one was joined one to another, and two covered their bodies. And they went everyone straight forward: whither the spirit was to go, they went; and they turned not when they went,"* [Ezekiel 1:3-12].

Satan defied God, the same God Ezekiel described, and we know what his end will be.

Proverbs the [*thirty-first chapter*], is as well, a compare/contrast example of a woman living a desirable life in God's sight and one who lives an undesirable life in God's sight.

The Proverbial Woman's race was, as is our race is, to Zion.

She ran her race faithfully each day, that not only was she be pleasing to her husband but was found pleasing to God.

The Proverbial Woman's focus was also on Heaven, looking to the day when she would hear '*well done My good and faithful servant.*' She did not allow herself to become physically weak during her peak years of life, nor did she not see the need for exercise. We see this by her constant activity.

The Proverbial Woman prepared for the eventuality of being old and she worked while she was young (**during our day**) because as times goes on age takes a toll and our bodies began to be less efficient and we suffer in our lives; we no longer can work at the same level, nor do we have the strength (**we come to our night**).

> ➤ **Your days will come to the years of the hoar head will your works speak for you as her works spoke for her?**

We run the race that is eternal in nature. Paul, the Apostle encouraged us in this manner, "*Know ye not that they which run in a race run all, but one receiveth the prize? So run, that ye may obtain. And every man that striveth for the mastery is temperate in all things. Now they do it to obtain a corruptible crown; but we incorruptible. I therefore so run, not as uncertainly; so, fight I, not as one that beateth the air: but I keep under my body, and bring it into subjection: lest that by any means, when I have preached to others, I myself should be a castaway,*" [I Corinthians 9:24-27].

Our race is to the finish line, the goal is ahead of us. Those miles we traveled faithfully puts us closer to our goals: and that is pleasing to God, and we will inherit Heaven, for all eternity.

The Proverbial Woman was dressed for the duties God commands and not undressed in slothfulness or negligence but dressed in the awareness that the time is at hand; the day of the Lord is near. She, overtime, continued to add to her spiritual dress in obedience and submission to the will of God.

We are to be found spiritually dressed and about the duties of the Christian Woman according to the will of God.

In the finality of Solomon's wisdom in Ecclesiastics, he teaches us in this manner, because age will bring this wisdom into focus: our bodies change, hair grows white, we do not stand as straight, our strength wains overtime, we lose our hearing, our teeth, our sight, therefore serving God when we are younger is wiser, age bring with it less tenacity and willingness to work; so we work while it is day (have our youth and strength in all things), "*Remember now thy Creator in the days of thy youth, while the evil days come not, nor the years draw nigh, when thou shalt say, "I have no pleasure in them; while the sun, or the light, or the moon, or the stars, be not darkened, nor the clouds return after the rain: in the day when the keepers of the house shall tremble, and the strong men shall bow themselves, and the grinders cease because they are few, and those that look out of the windows be darkened, and the doors shall be shut in the streets, when the sound of the grinding is low, and he shall rise up at the voice of the bird, and all the daughters of musick shall be brought low;"*

"Also, when they shall be afraid of that which is high, and fears shall be in the way, and the almond tree shall flourish, and the grasshopper shall be a burden, and desire shall fail: because man goeth to his long home, and the mourners go about the streets: or ever the silver cord be loosed, or the golden bowl be broken, or the pitcher be broken at the fountain, or the wheel broken at the cistern,"

"Then shall the dust return to the earth as it was: and the spirit shall return unto God who gave it. Vanity of vanities, saith the Preacher; all is vanity. And moreover, because the preacher was wise, he still taught the people knowledge; yea, he gave good heed, and sought out, and set in order many proverbs,"

"The preacher sought to find out acceptable words: and that which was written was upright, even words of truth. The words of the wise are as goads, and as nails fastened by the masters of assemblies, which are given from one shepherd. And further, by these, my son, be admonished: of making many books there is no end; and much study is a weariness of the flesh. Let us hear the conclusion of the whole matter: Fear God and keep His commandments: for this is the whole duty of man. For God shall bring every work into judgment, with every secret thing, whether it be good, or whether it be evil," [Ecclesiastics 12:1-14].

As well, we can be assured of the same promise God gave Abraham and with the unwavering confidence that [He] will never break any covenant [He] makes with [His] people. [He] was for Abraham as [He] is for us, our shield if we live as Abraham lived in a pleasing manner before [Him], *"After these things the word of the Lord came unto Abram in a vision, saying, Fear not, Abram: I am thy shield, and thy exceeding great reward,"* [Genesis 15:1].

Isaiah gives us a perfect description of the Holy God Whom we serve, *"Behold, the Lord God will come with strong hand, and [His] arm shall rule for[Him]: behold, [His] reward is with [Him], and [His] work before [Him]. [He] shall feed [His] flock like a shepherd: [He] shall gather the lambs with [His] arm, and carry them in [His] bosom, and shall gently lead those that are with young. Who hath measured the waters in the hollow of [His] hand, and meted out heaven with the span, and comprehended the dust of the earth in a measure, and weighed the mountains in scales, and the hills in a balance? Who hath directed the Spirit of the Lord, or being [His] counsellor hath taught [Him]?" [Isaiah 40:10-13].*

"Have ye not known? have ye not heard? hath it not been told you from the beginning? have ye not understood from the foundations of the earth? It is [He] that sitteth upon the circle of the earth, and the inhabitants thereof are as grasshoppers; that stretcheth out the heavens as a curtain, and spreadeth them out as a tent to dwell in: That bringeth the princes to nothing; [He] maketh the judges of the earth as vanity. Yea, they shall not be planted; yea, they shall not be sown, yea their stock shall not take root in the earth: and [He] shall also blow upon them, and they shall wither, and the whirlwind shall take them away as stubble. To whom then will ye liken [Me], or shall I be equal? saith the Holy One," [Isaiah 40:21-25].

"Lift up your eyes on high, and behold who hath created these things, that bringeth out their hosts by number: [He] calleth them all by names by the greatness of [Hi]s might, for that [He] is strong in power; not one faileth. Why sayest thou, O Jacob, and speakest, O Israel, my way is hidden from the Lord, and my judgment is passed over from my God? Hast thou not known? hast thou not heard that the everlasting God, the Lord, the Creator of the ends of the earth, fainteth not, neither is weary? there is no searching of [His] understanding. [He] giveth power to the faint; and to them that have no might [He] increaseth strength. Even the youths shall faint and be weary, and the young men shall utterly fall: But they that wait upon the Lord shall renew their strength; they shall mount up with wings as eagles; they shall run, and not be weary; and they shall walk, and not faint," [Isaiah 40:26-31].

Jacob erected an alter to the *El-elohe-Israel* (God, the God of Israel) in the field that he purchased so that he might worship Him in the manner commanded. He is still the Mighty God; the Creator; we are to praise His name and rejoice that He loves and cares for us on our sojourn to the eternal Canaan, *"And he bought a parcel of a field, where he had spread his tent, at the hand of the children of Hamor, Shechem's father, for a hundred pieces of money. And he erected there an altar and called it El-elohe-Israel," [Genesis 33:19-20].*

God is still the God of the Spiritual Israel!

The Psalmist wrote of the dangers of desiring the life lived in the world and not for God. Even the strongest of Christians can slip if they are not careful.

Envy of the pleasures of the world is not to be found among the people of God, a King, or leader. Their desire and love for the riches of the world leads to destruction.

Sinful appetites lead men to uncontrollable cravings; them being ruled by their own determination and desire, doing what pleases them, as we read of in the actions of the strange and adulterous woman and examples of others given in Scripture whose fancy and strong will – will lead them to an end of eternal destruction.

Job the [*thirty-nineth chapter*]expresses sin using beast: the Wild Ass wandering about with no direction; the Ostrich with no wisdom or understanding; the Unicorn unwilling to serve; the horse with no fear; but runs headlong into the battle; and the Eagle with sharp eyes that dwell among the heights of the rocks, *[Job 39:1-27]*.

We cannot indulge in sin as with the Ostrich with no wisdom who forsake her young; or the Wild Ass wandering with no direction; those who hearts are hardened does not fear God like the horse running toward a bloody battle. There is no safety in sin from the power of God. Man was given by God, the power of understanding, the ability to discern, to choose to obey, or live in danger of eternal retribution from the Creator.

> ➤ **When God asked Job those questions about things to high for the mind of man, he could not answer, can we?**

Jeremiah, the Prophet, tells us the results of those who practice defiance and disobedience, when plunging headlong into the desires of their hearts with no fear or regard for the commands of God, with mindless wandering, lack of wisdom, harden hearts, they are not safe in their sins, *"Thy terribleness hath deceived thee and the pride of thine heart though thy dwelleth in the cleft of rocks that holdest the heights of the hill: though thy shouldest make thy nest as high as the eagle, I will bring you down from thence, saith the Lord," [Jeremiah 49:16]*.

God asked Job, *"Shall he that contendeth with the Almighty instruct Him? He that reproveth God let him answer Him," [Job 40:2]*.

Hear the wisdom of Job when he answered the Almighty, *"Behold, I am vile! What shall I answer thee? I will lay mine hand upon my mouth," [Job 40:4]*.

It is wise to take the position of Job and the Proverbial Woman that God be pleased with us. We are not stronger, wiser, nor more powerful than He no matter how we view ourselves.

God declared His Power to Job through questions and declarative statements:

"Wilt thou also disannul my judgment? wilt thou condemn Me, that thou mayest be righteous?" [Job 40:8].

"Hast thou an arm like God? or canst thou thunder with a voice like Him?" [Job 40:9]

"Deck thyself now with majesty and excellency; and array thyself with glory and beauty," [Job 40:10].

"Cast abroad the rage of thy wrath: and behold every one that is proud, and abase him," [Job 40:11].

"Look on every one that is proud and bring him low; and tread down the wicked in their place," [Job 40:12].

"Hide them in the dust together; and bind their faces in secret," [Job 40:13].

Hear the sum of God's Power as He spoke with Job, *"Then will I also confess unto thee that thine own right hand can save thee," [Job 40:14]*.

David reminds us, when involved with or envious of the wicked of the world and is confident that God does not see or know the ways of their life, and their mouths, and minds are set against Heaven and the God of all creation, who is all-knowing, all-seeing, and all-hearing that, *"Truly God is good to Israel, even to such as are of a clean heart. But as for me, my feet were almost gone; my steps had well-nigh slipped. For I was envious at the foolish when I saw the prosperity of the wicked. For there are no bands in their death: but their strength is firm. They are not in trouble as other men; neither are they plagued like other men. Therefore, pride compasseth them about as a chain; violence covereth them as a garment. Their eyes stand out with fatness: they have more than the heart could wish. They are corrupt and speak wickedly concerning oppression: they speak loftily. They set their mouth against the heavens, and their tongue walketh through the earth. Therefore, His people return hither: and waters of a full cup are wrung out to them. And they say, how doth God know? and is there knowledge in the Most High? Behold, these are the ungodly, who prosper in the world; they increase in riches," [Psalms 73:1-12]*.

The end of the wicked as the Psalmist reminds us, is as thus, "*Until I went into the sanctuary of God; then understood I, their end. Surely, thou didst set them in slippery places: thou castedst them down into destruction. How are they brought into desolation, as in a moment! they are utterly consumed with terrors. As a dream when one awaketh, so, O Lord, when thou awakest, thou shalt despise their image,*" [Psalms 73:17-20].

The Psalmist understood the end of wickedness and the security of the faithful, "*Nevertheless I am continually with thee: thou hast holden me by my right hand. Thou shalt guide me with thy counsel, and afterward receive me to glory. Whom have I in heaven but thee? and there is none upon earth that I desire beside thee. My flesh and my heart faileth: but God are the strength of my heart, and my portion forever. For, lo, they that are far from thee shall perish: thou hast destroyed all of them that go a whoring from thee,*" [Psalms 73:22-27].

He understood why it is wisdom to draw near to God, "*But it is good for me to draw near to God: I have put my trust in the Lord God, that I may declare all Thy works,*" [Psalms 73:28].

The Psalmist said, "My steps well-nigh slipped. Fire will weaken the strongest of iron if it is heated long enough. Regardless how strong we are, if we cannot depend upon God for strength and resilience our steps will slip. Man within himself and by his self is inherently weak and foot can and will slip if we do not walk circumspectly. Awareness is necessary on our sojourn. We are in a war, a spiritual war with Satan for our souls. He is competing for our souls and will win if we are not careful. Our steps can slip and will slip.

The Psalmist said, "nigh-slipped." The Proverbial Woman stayed within the confines of the Laws of God. Though she had daily challenges, overcame each of them day-by-day and stayed on course. The challenges she faced and the battles she had in just her everyday life we can identify with. She worked and overcame each of them, as we can if we put our dependence upon our God and Savior and stay faithful.

Jesus promised, "*In this world you will have tribulation, but be of good cheer I have overcome the world,*" [Ibid].

There is nothing we face in this world God cannot help us overcome as the Proverbial Woman knew. Yet again, as Paul reminds us, "*There hath no temptation taken you, but such as is common to man: but God is faithful, who will not suffer you to be tempted above that ye are able; but will with the temptation also make a way to escape, that ye may be able to bear it,*" [I Corinthians 10:13].

God gives us a way out and a path to get through the challenges we face. Our faith and hope should never leave us though it gets weak, but we hang on as the Hebrew writer tell us that, *"Faith is the substance of things hoped for and the evidence of things not seen,"* [Hebrews 11:1].

The second verse of the Eleventh Chapter of Hebrews reminds us of not only the elders spoken of here but the Proverbial Woman's success in overcoming this life's challenges, *"For by [it] the elders obtained a good report,"* [Hebrews 11:1] and, *"Many daughters have done virtuously, but thou excellest them all,"* [Proverbs 31:29].

The [it] spoken of here is Faith. Our faith is the substance, the meat of our belief. We cannot please God without the substance. We hope and have faith in His promises though we do not see the promise but know and believe He is faithful who promised.

The Proverbial Woman had the same hope and faith in the God she served. We are serving the same God and those promises are there if we continue in the substance with hope alive.

The Psalmist came to this realization before his steps slipped and turned his focus from the people of the world with wealth and success, as we must before our steps nigh-slip.

> ➤ **Abraham was willing to let go of his only son Isaac. What do you love the most in this world that you can give up because God asked that we put him first in all things having no other god before Him? What is your Isaac?**

The currents of life will take you off course if we do not remain aware. The Proverbial Woman stayed anchored in God with her faith strong and her resolve even stronger.

Paul warns us to, *"Beware lest any man spoil you through philosophy and vain deceit, after the tradition of men, after the rudiments of the world, and not after Christ. For in Him dwelleth all the fulness of the Godhead bodily. And ye are complete in Him, which is the Head of all principality and power,"* [Colossians 2:8-10].

What is most important is having our hearts approved of God as did the Proverbial Woman and not being overly concerned about what man thinks of us. The Scripture tell us it is better to please God than to please man.

The Proverbial Woman's reputation stood for her down through the ages. If our ways are pleasing to God and we live a righteous life, He will make even our enemies to be at peace with us, *"When a man's ways please the Lord, He maketh even his enemies to be at peace with him. Better is a little with righteousness than great revenues without right," [Proverbs 16:7-8].*

The Word of God is life unto life or death unto death; the Proverbial Woman knew this, as we should, and should choose, as she did, life unto life.

We are reminded today, *"Be not carried about with divers and strange doctrine: for it is a good thing that the heart be established with grace; not with meat, which have not profited them that have been occupied therein," [Hebrews 13:9].*

When God sent Ezekiel to the rebellious house of Israel warned him that men are wicked but be not afraid of their words but deliver the prophecy, though their words are like briers, thorns, and he was among scorpions, because they are rebellious. These characteristics must not be found or named among God's people, *"And thou, son of man, be not afraid of them, neither be afraid of their words, though briers and thorns be with thee, and thou dost dwell among scorpions: be not afraid of their words, nor be dismayed at their looks, though they be a rebellious house," [Ezekiel 2:6].*

God was with Ezekiel and is with us as obedient children. He promised to never leave us alone, *"The angel of the Lord encampeth round about them that fear Him, and delivereth them," [Psalms 34:7].*

We do not see any of the negative characteristics in the Proverbial Woman that God saw in the people of Israel that Ezekiel delivered the Prophecy to from God.

Though people may not like or care for you, they will respect you and the fact that you choose to live a righteous life. We are to please God, not man nor ourselves.

Paul encourages us to go forward as Ezekiel did, *"That ye be not soon shaken in mind, or be troubled, neither by spirit, nor by word, nor by letter as from us, as that the day of Christ is at hand," [2 Thessalonians 2:4].*

"Our God is a consuming fire," [Hebrews 12:29].

We are to separate from: the world, from sin, and from ourselves.

As we see the life of the Proverbial Woman was pleasing to God, so can it be in our life. We will not suffer long on this earth, but after we have faithfully gone through the fires and trials of this world will live forever with those decisions, we made to serve God. Serving Christ in faith renders peace, which we cannot obtain in this world. Our sacrifices should be to God through our life and faithfulness to His commands, not as the world deems, but Jesus Christ, whose blood purchased our Salvation, *"But by Him therefore, let us offer the sacrifice of praise to God continually, that is the fruit of our lips giving thanks to His name. But to do good and communicate forget not: for with such sacrifices God is well pleased," [Hebrews 13:15-16].*

God is still the shield and exceeding great reward of His people, *"I am your shield, your exceedingly great reward," [Genesis 15:1].*

Paul tells us we are serving Jesus Christ, *"Who is the image of the invisible God, the firstborn of every creature: for by [Him] were all things created, that are in heaven, and that are in earth, visible and invisible, whether they be thrones, or dominions, or principalities, or powers: all things were created by [Him], and for [Him]: and [He] is before all things, and by [Him] all things consist. And [He] is the [Head] of the Body, the Church: [Who] is the beginning, the Firstborn from the dead; that in all things [He] might have the preeminence," [Colossians 1:15-18].*

"The Spirit Himself bears witness with our spirit that we are children of God, and if children, then heirs—heirs of God and joint heirs with Christ, if indeed we suffer with Him, that we may also be glorified together," [Romans 8:16-17].

Our suffering here is but for a moment in time compared to the joy of eternity before us, *"For I reckon that the sufferings of this present time are not worthy to be compared with the glory which shall be revealed in us," [Romans 8:18].*

The Proverbial Woman had the same hope for an eternity of peace with God that we do as Paul ask, do we wait for it with patience? *"For we are saved by hope: but hope that is seen is not hope: for what a man seeth, why doth he yet hope for? But if we hope for that we see not, then do we with patience wait for it?" [Romans 8:24-25].*

Christians now and servants of God then knows and knew, *"For I am persuaded, that neither death, nor life, nor angels, nor principalities, nor powers, nor things present, nor things to come, nor height, nor depth, nor any other creature, shall be able to separate us from the love of God, which is in Christ Jesus our Lord," [Romans 8:38-39].*

> ### The choice we make the world or Christ is what will govern our lives: What will that choice be?

Humans will make provisions in their lives to live within their choices. Freedom to choose is before us, *"And if it seems evil unto you to serve the Lord, choose you this day whom ye will serve," [Joshua 24:15].*

"Jesus is the same yesterday, today, and forever," [Hebrews 13:8].

¡Amen!

BIBLIOGRAPHY

Curruptio Optimi Pessima:
https://www.merriam-webster.com/dictionary/corruptio optimi pessima

Dictionary:
http://www.dictionary.com

English Standard Version (ESV):
https://www.biblestudytools.com/esv

King James Study Bible (KJV) [Holman: 2012
King James Bible (KJV) 2000
King James Bible: kingjamesbibleonline.org

Life Application Study Bible:
New Living Translation (NLT): 3rd ed. 2019

Life Application Study Bible:
New Living Translation (NLT) 4th ed. 2011

Matthew Henry Commentary (1710):
https://www.biblestudytools.com/commentaries/matthew-henry-complete

New International Version (NIV)
https://www.bible.com/versions/111

Webster Dictionary:
https://www.merriam-webster.com.